DRAMAS

Worship Feast

15 Sketches for Youth Group, Worship, & More

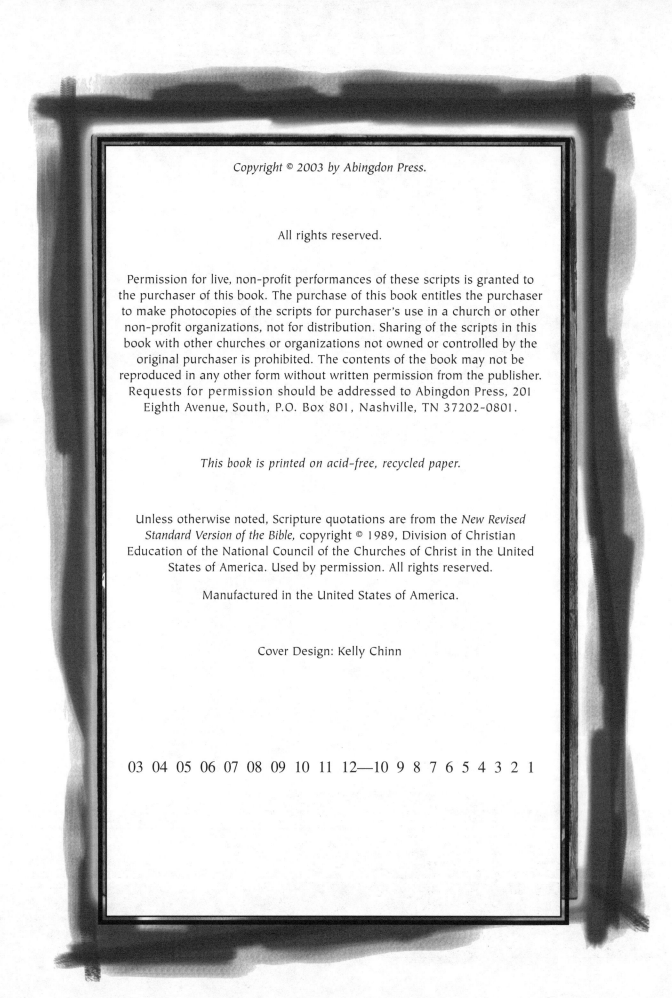

Cover Design: Kelly Chinn

03 04 05 06 07 08 09 10 11 12—10 9 8 7 6 5 4 3 2 1

Worship Feast

15 Sketches for Youth Group, Worship, & More

DRAMAS

the Strangely Warmed Players

CONTENTS

Introduction: How to Use This Book

The essence of drama is that it must reach the heart. Good drama engages both the mind and the emotions. It stirs the imagination and sparks a search for meaning. When choosing a name for our touring drama ensemble, we wanted a name that would reflect both the group's Wesleyan heritage and the ability of drama to touch lives, provoke thought, and initiate change.

John Wesley, the founder of Methodism, was on Aldersgate Street in London one evening in 1738. Although he had preached, prayed, and studied the Bible for years, Wesley had a profound spiritual experience that night. Wesley described the encounter in his diary: "In the evening I went very unwillingly to a society, where one was reading Luther's preface to the Epistle to the Romans. About a quarter before nine, while he was describing the change which God works in the heart through faith in Christ, I felt my heart strangely warmed." (From the *Journal of John Wesley* for May 14, 1738)

"Strangely warmed" reflects both our faith tradition and our objective of offering the opportunity for transformation. Thus, the name we chose for the troupe was The Strangely Warmed Players. Just as Wesley had a passion for reaching the common people with the message of God's love and transforming power, The Strangely Warmed Players attempt to bring Christ's message through contemporary drama. The primary purpose is for audiences to experience faith-warmed hearts through drama.

Worship Feast: Dramas includes both information about doing drama and scripts for dramatic presentations. The scripts have been performed in worship services, youth rallies, evening youth meetings, public schools, mission boards, Sunday school classes, Bible studies, women's meetings, banquets, nursing homes, camps. They have even been performed on mission trips. In addition, they have been used for evenings set aside specifically for drama performance. They appeal to teenagers, children, adults, senior citizens . . . and even youth leaders.

> The essence of drama is that it must reach the heart. Good drama engages both the mind and the emotions. It stirs the imagination and sparks a search for meaning.

The scripts are from the repertoire of The Strangely Warmed Players. The global appeal of the scripts was evident at the 2001 World Methodist Conference in Brighton, England, and at the International Christian Youth Conference in 2002 at the University of Ulster, in Northern Ireland. But don't let that discourage you—most of these sketches have also been performed by inexperienced junior high youth.

Chapter 1 explores the rationale for doing drama in the church and provides some answers to the question, "Why drama?" You are invited to discover your own reasons for doing drama.

Chapter 2, "Starting on the Upstage Foot," contains brief suggestions on staging; the director's role; tryouts; rehearsals, including schedules; acting techniques; and basic stage movement.

The scripts are divided into three groupings. Each script has an introductory page with a list of suggested costumes and props, the number of characters, and the setting. The theme or Scripture reference is given. Background information about how and why the sketch was written is included, along with brief director's notes. Each introductory page also has several questions for group discussion about the play. This feature expands the use of the scripts and provides an additional teaching tool.

Chapter 3 contains eight thematic sketches. Each sketch is two to six minutes long. These require minimal or no props or costumes. They can be used in any setting. The final script is an example of how a drama sketch can be used to enhance an announcement for fundraising.

> "Strangely warmed" reflects both our faith tradition and our objective of offering the opportunity for transformation.

Chapter 4 includes six slightly longer, Scripture sketches. Each of these sketches is a contemporary portrayal of Scripture. They are ten to eighteen minutes long. Minimal props and costumes are needed; however, you can do them without costuming.

Chapter 5 contains a Christmas play, "Chicken Soup at the Bethlehem Inn." It is about forty-five minutes long. Although the script is written for thirty-seven persons, you can cast it with as few as fifteen if you eliminate some scenes and/or double cast. Biblical costumes are recommended, but you could perform it in a contemporary setting if you choose. We rewrite this play each year to accommodate every senior high youth who wants a part and who commits to rehearsal.

We hope that as you perform these plays, the hearts of your audience members are strangely warmed.

—Beth Miller, Director
The Strangely Warmed Players

Chapter 1: Why Drama?

Before you use drama in a Christian setting, ask yourself, "Why do I want to use drama?" Drama, like preaching, can be a powerful tool for transformation. However, drama is abstract and more multisensory; it evokes not just thought but feeling. A statement by a seminary professor more than thirty years ago has stuck with me. He said; "If you can say it better in a sermon, do so." Drama is implicit; sermons are explicit.

Misuse of drama in the church includes a sort of sledgehammer approach. The message is too obvious. I once saw a Christian drama troupe where every character quoted the Bible or actually stated the message of the play. Each of their sketches included a Christ figure; and at the conclusion, someone was converted, in the traditional sense of the word. In a couple of the plays, a character actually preached. I felt that they were attempting to tell the whole gospel at once. Rarely are these expressions true to life. Often they feel like a bad Christian soap opera.

The plays in this book were written to help the audience ask the right questions, not to provide all of the answers. The sketches should stimulate opinions and attitudes that lead to renewal. More direct forms of communication, such as preaching and Bible studies, are far better at delivering information. These plays were written to wake up the audience, to provide an "ah-ha," or evoke an uncomfortable laugh. The scripts are tools for communicating the Word. They offer another venue for touching the heart, another means of transformation.

> Why you decide to do drama will determine the type of play you choose, the actors you select, how you direct, and the audiences for whom you perform.

Why you decide to do drama will determine the type of play you choose, the actors you select, how you direct, and the audiences for whom you perform. Although many reasons are valid for doing drama in church, the ones below are foundational for me.

DRAMA PROVIDES AN EXPERIENCE OF THE HEART

For those who know the gospel well, drama can provide fresh insight, another view, and an experience of the heart. The Strangely Warmed Players had just finished performing "The Prodigal Son" at a small church in north central England. At teatime, following the performance, the clergyperson pointed out what she described as a rare sight: two gentlemen shaking hands and sharing a lively conversation. What was so unusual about that? I know that the British have a reputation for being reserved, but this exchange didn't seem extraordinary.

As it turned out, these two church stewards hadn't spoken to each other in more than a year. They had had a disagreement over church policy. The pastor had preached several sermons on reconciliation and had even brought in a denominational mediator, to no avail. I was nervous as the gentlemen approached. A common foe often brings together the worst enemies. Perhaps they thought that our humor was inappropriate for worship? The Lord works in mysterious ways. I took a deep breath and listened. The elder of the two explained, through misty eyes, that in the midst of the performance, he was overwhelmed with the need to forgive his brother. The famous Greek philosopher Aristotle described the experience of drama as catharsis, a purging of the emotions.

DRAMA CAN COMMUNICATE ETERNAL TRUTHS

Jesus used the power of story to communicate eternal truths. In addition to preaching and teaching, Christ also told stories, parables. His stories were much different from his preaching. Parables are not true in the sense of being factual, but they embody truth. Drama is another form of story. The story might not be true, but it must be real enough to convincingly surprise the audience. The audience must be able to identify with the characters and action in the play. Sometimes preparation is needed for the type of drama you are using, especially in the church. If humor is not a usual part of worship and you are performing a funny sketch, remember to say so in the introduction. Give the audience permission to laugh.

The opposite is also true, if you are portraying a serious matter, you may wish to alert your audience. Our troupe learned this the hard way. The youth were giving a series of serious monologues written about painful experiences. Kim, who in real life was the homecoming queen, portrayed a homecoming queen who used purging to keep slim and beautiful. Following the performance, a woman thanked her for her courage in admitting her eating disorder and sharing it with the congregation. She prayed that Kim's story would make it easier for someone else to seek help. Kim shared that prayer but didn't tell the woman that she was just acting and had never had an eating disorder. Branden was worried after that performance because his character had admitted to using drugs and alcohol.

> *Drama is another form of story. The story might not be true, but it must be real enough to convincingly surprise the audience.*

DRAMA IS A POWERFUL VENUE FOR OUTREACH

Drama is a powerful venue for outreach, presenting the reality of God's presence and revealing Christ's nature. For the biblically illiterate, hearing the gospel for the first time through drama can provoke interest, hunger, and acceptance. Our troupe did a series of assemblies, followed by drama workshops, at schools in England. At one particular school not far from Bristol, the head master introduced the troupe, explaining that we were a United Methodist youth group touring the U.K. Most of the students had heard of John Wesley from British history. Our performance for the older, high school aged students included "The Prodigal Son." The head master asked the assembled students how many of them were familiar with this story. Not one hand was raised. He then asked the students whether they had questions for the group about the plays we had just presented.

The subsequent dialogue was incredible. One young man found it absolutely implausible that the father of the prodigal son represented God. "Do you really know that God is that forgiving?" he asked. "Absolutely!" cast members responded. The questions came like wildfire. The dramas provided a spontaneous and sincere opportunity for faith sharing. After school, many of students came back to the auditorium to talk with the cast and exchange e-mail addresses. The head master was pleased. Our subtle approach was very effective in reaching a group of unchurched young persons. The plays portrayed theological concepts that were new and convincing.

DRAMA CAN BE TRANSFORMING

Drama can quickly get to the depth of meaning, the significance of our experiences. Drama has a feeling tone. Acting out the Bible is much more compelling than reading the Bible. The process of characterization requires empathy with each role. It develops compassion and sensitivity to others. It requires responsiveness and thwarts greed, apathy, or cynicism.

On a winter ski retreat, the youth group worshiped at a local country church. The text for the day was John 2:1-11, the wedding at Cana. "Wendell's Wonderful Weddings" had been part of our repertoire for ten years. Everyone in this group had either watched several performances or portrayed one of the roles. The youth exchanged knowing looks and nudges as the Scripture was being read. Garrison, who had portrayed the servant, mouthed, "There were six stone water jars . . . each holding three firkins." Megan repeated, "Woman, my time has not yet come." At this point, several youth could not contain their giggles, recalling our interpretation of the story and Mary's response to Jesus. Nathan, as Wendell, the wedding consultant, had the lines, "Everyone serves the good wine first. . . ."

> *Drama has a feeling tone. Acting out the Bible is much more compelling than reading the Bible.*

After the service, the minister commented that the group seemed very attentive to the story. I apologized for the giggles and explained why they related to the narrative. Two things were apparent: The group not only knew the Scripture, to the point of having most of it memorized, but they knew the story intimately. They knew the details of the story, and they understood the meaning. They identified with the characters. Acting facilitates becoming part of the story in an unforgettable way.

Actors experience vicariously the story they are telling. Good acting requires the actor to create believable characters on stage. Stanislavski, the renowned Russian actor and director from the 1800s, taught that acting is "Thinking the right thoughts." Acting is not feeling the part but thinking the thoughts of the character you are portraying.

DRAMA CAN BE A POWERFUL TEACHING TOOL

I will often intentionally cast someone in a role that is contrary to his or her personality. The challenge of creating a character different from oneself pushes the actor to stretch and go deeper. This method helps good actors become better. Two brothers, Joshua and Nathan, were preparing "The Prodigal Son." Nathan, the eldest, was the one more likely to push the boundaries. Nathan was not an overachiever; however, Joshua was. Joshua was cast as the prodigal son, and Nathan was cast as the elder brother.

Joshua reported that he was uncomfortable with the way the other characters in the play began to treat him. He wasn't used to being the wild one, the one breaking the rules. At one point on the tour, he had a serious disagreement with the person playing the father. As the director, I was concerned about that evening's performance. Harmony among the cast was important—not only for the performance, but for living closely together in Christian community. My concern was expressed through private prayer. The forgiveness scene between the father and the prodigal son that night was provocative and compelling. Thinking the right thoughts for the characters they were portraying led the actors to real forgiveness. The tears were genuine—as was the forgiveness. The action of the play touched the hearts of the actors and the audience that night.

Portraying characters on stage can help actors develop tolerance for persons who are different from them. Anna is a straight-A student, the captain of the varsity basketball team at her private school, president of her class, an active church member, and a leading actress in the drama troupe. One of her most believable performances was that of a loner rejected by her peers, a person used to losing, messing up, and failure. After playing that part, Anna expressed how she is more aware of others who fall into this stereotype. She has more compassion for what they must be feeling, and she works to reach out to them in meaningful ways. When portraying someone else, an actor cannot remain objective; an actor must attempt subjectivity. Acting encourages persons to develop an appreciation of, a compassion for, and a respect for others.

> *Portraying characters on stage can help actors develop tolerance for persons who are different from them.*

DRAMA IS AN EXCELLENT TEAM BUILDER

Rather than focus on "Are my needs being met?", acting forces the cast to work for the good of the whole. Putting together an ensemble troupe each year to produce these sketches is an amazing process. The youth are usually from five or more high schools, from different grades, and not close friends. Variety in appearance and temperament is important for casting. Members of The Strangely Warmed Players are not chosen for their dramatic talent. The criteria include dramatic potential (difficult to estimate), willingness to commit to a rigorous rehearsal schedule to produce a high-quality acting troupe, maturity, flexibility, ability to get along with others and take direction, and commitment to the Christian faith that includes intentional participation in faith growing opportunities. Each troupe has become a wonderful Christian community. As the youth become more comfortable with themselves, they also learn to be more open and responsive to others.

On one trip, a cast member was unable to participate; so Megan Jo met us at the airport with her scripts. She had not been part of the six months of rehearsal preparing for our Ireland tour. Megan Jo was younger than the others and attended a different school in another city. The group was acquainted with Megan Jo from youth group but didn't really know her. Megan Jo was an introvert, eager to be a part of this particular tour but feeling overwhelmed and not connected with the troupe.

The last-minute addition of a new actor demanded intense rehearsal time wherever it could be found. A three-hour layover at the Toronto airport was our first rehearsal opportunity. The six other cast members encouraged and commended Megan Jo. On the plane, the group rehearsed their lines. The group felt as much of a responsibility to Megan Jo as she did to the troupe to present the best drama we could for the glory of our Creator God. Megan Jo was hesitant, holding back even from group photos. The others drew her into the group at every opportunity.

Megan Jo later described this tour as a life-changing experience. She developed deep friendships with fellow cast members. The process of rehearsals, the experience of performing, and the seeking of a common purpose within a Christian community provided a means for fellowship and inspiration. A drama team with Christian values at their core can provide a setting for spiritual and personal growth. Acceptance, non-competition, and respect for each individual in the group is important. Trust is an imperative element for a good ensemble troupe.

Actors who are committed to achieving excellence and growing in their performing skills encourage one another to be exceptional. I've too often heard a group's excuse for not learning lines and giving a mediocre performance—"It's only for church." Performing during worship should be what motivates us to do our best. Drama in worship is an offering to God. Using our finest creativity and talent seems a reasonable and appropriate goal. Giving our best is an act of gratitude to the Giver of our talents.

DRAMA CAN BUILD SELF-ESTEEM AND CONFIDENCE

Casting is a delicate process. Actors need to be challenged but not overwhelmed. Casting for success, not only for the play but for the individual, is important. Each role should build the actors' self-assurance and ability. Catriona was, at first, a reluctant player. She never sought lead roles. Happy to be part of the troupe, she was quite satisfied with minor roles. Besides, the saying that "There are no small parts" was ingrained into our group's collective psyche. Slowly, Catriona became more and more creative with very small parts. A turning point came in Catriona's acting as if a light had been turned on. I sensed a newly found freedom of expression in her performance one night on tour, a confidence on stage that came after years of performance. This seems to come to each committed actor in his or her own time. A year later, watching her perform a lead role before an international audience of thousands, I was overcome with tears. She had the entire audience in the palm of her hand. Her performance was electrifying, superb. The entire cast was on the money and deserved the standing ovation they received. It was one of life's meaningful moments.

Deep within every person is a fundamental need for creative expression. The arts provide activities for emotional release and stimulation of the imagination. In the beginning, God created; perhaps when we are able to create, to imagine, we are relating to the nature of God.

> Drama in worship is an offering to God. Giving our best is an act of gratitude to the Giver of our talents.

DRAMA CAN TEACH PROBLEM-SOLVING SKILLS

Not only do actors learn communication skills and confidence in presenting ideas and information, but they learn new problem-solving skills. No two performances are ever alike. I have an unbreakable rule against breaking character. Actors are expected to thoroughly learn all of the lines, not just their own. Even the best of actors forgets a line when it is least expected. Training the ensemble how to respond to a dropped line is important. Actors must never mouth the line to the person who dropped the line. Good actors know how to say the dropped line, rephrasing to fit their character. Good actors listen and respond in character, ad-libbing or cutting part of the script and going on. Some of the best performances come when something goes wrong and the members of the cast, while staying in character, resolve the problem.

In the final performance of one of our England tours, we were at a small church in Derbyshire. Our hosts were a warm, enthusiastic congregation. Everything was going wrong that night; it was indeed our "grand finale." It seems that Gabriel's angel costume for "In Those Days" was left at the Brighton Convention Centre, miles from where we were. Megan thought to ask the pastor whether they might borrow a white acolyte robe. Voilá, instant angel! Joshua's Wendell moustache finally gave out during his first scene, falling off in front of the audience. It was absurd but hilarious when he returned for the second scene with a full beard, borrowed from Zechariah. To this day I don't know exactly what went wrong during "The Prodigal Son." When they got to the part where the Fatted Calf was to sing a light aria before her death, the pigs returned; and the next thing I knew, the cast had the entire congregation singing "Old Macdonald Had a Farm." What a memorable night! What fun!

Why drama? Why not! Open your group to new ways to communicate the gospel. The stories may have inspired you while providing some compelling reasons for doing drama. Give it a go. Grab a script and start rehearsing. Perhaps reading these scripts will inspire you to write your own. Listen to the Holy Spirit. Discover your gifts. Recruit some live bodies and have fun!

What do actors gain from the process of doing drama?

- ☐▶ Confidence—in their abilities and in others
- ☐▶ Communication skills—grow in their ability to communicate not only verbally but also with their bodies, their thoughts, and their feelings.
- ☐▶ Control—movement, voice, body, characterization, thoughts
- ☐▶ Cooperation—develop a strong sense of teamwork and connectedness.
- ☐▶ Comfortable—being in front of others, with themselves.
- ☐▶ Creativity—develop imagination, problem-solving skills, and ingenuity
- ☐▶ Christian doctrine and beliefs—The dramatic material chosen should be a springboard for developing the actor's faith, core beliefs, and actions.

> *Open your group to new ways to communicate the gospel.*

Chapter 2:
Starting on the Upstage Foot

If you are new to drama ministry or new to drama, in general, this chapter can be particularly helpful. Drama ministry should not be separate from but a complement to the other ministries of the church. When drama is incorporated with worship, the worship experience can become more meaningful. Therefore, the drama coordinator should work with the worship team or senior pastor to find times appropriate to include drama in corporate worship.

Some youth groups have a drama coordinator and several directors, depending upon the play or skit being performed. Other youth groups have just one director, who also coordinates the drama ministry. Some churches have a drama coordinator and director for adult drama ministry and a separate coordinator/director for youth drama ministry. Other churches have a drama ministry team that makes decisions and rotates the director duties. This chapter uses the model of only one director who is the primary person responsible for coordinating drama ministry in the church.

DIRECTOR'S ROLE

A good director provides support, security, affirmation, and nurture. The director's goal should be to bring out the best in each individual actor, to help each one reach his or her potential. When the actors realize that the director truly cares for them, they will discover an atmosphere where they can be nourished and grow. A philosopher once said, "One can teach only whom one loves." Only when the director accepts the youth in Christian love will a non-threatening environment be created where free expression and imaginative interpretation can take place.

> Drama ministry should not be separate from but a complement to the other ministries of the church.

Beginning rehearsals should be teaching sessions for the entire group, with little or no individual correction. As much as possible, give directions to the entire cast rather than to one individual. You can, however, ask an individual's permission to use him or her as an example for the entire cast to learn a technique. Also, be sure to focus on what the actors are doing right. Nothing stifles creativity as fast as criticism. Degrading remarks have no place. As the actors begin to trust the director and feel affirmed for their efforts, they will become more receptive to correction.

Although good directors are supportive and nurturing, they are also demanding. Remind the actors that it is your job to help them improve. Be sure they know that if you push them or ask them to do something again, it is only because you see potential in them to be better.

Patience is a valuable trait for all directors. Good actors evolve with experience over time. Youth who come to act in church performances may have been rejected by school productions. As a director, you have the opportunity to open a whole new world to students and to build their self-confidence as they develop their communication skills. What a thrill to see a student come alive on stage.

Do not allow cast members to direct or critique one another. Make it clear that you do the directing. Cast members are expected to encourage and respect one another and to appreciate everyone's abilities. The director's job is to build a team. Commend and demand. A good director knows when to offer blankets and when to administer sandpaper.

PRAYER

Undergird your drama ministry with prayer. Ask members of the congregation to pray for your drama ministry. Begin each rehearsal with devotions and prayer. The devotions can be a Bible study on the theme of your play.

> *Undergird your drama ministry with prayer. Ask members of the congregation to pray for your drama ministry.*

TRYOUTS/CASTING

Deciding who will perform which part is often the director's most difficult task. When multiple people want the same part, the director has to decide which one gets it. Most directors will hold tryouts and award the part to the person who performs best during the tryout. Being a Christian group, however, you might also want to consider who needs the affirmation, how you are growing your drama ministry for the future, and who has a full plate from other activities (school, work, recreation).

Sometimes when youth hear the word *tryouts*, they are so intimidated they will not even come. When you advertise tryouts say, "This is a chance for you to try out the play to see whether it is one you want to be in. This is a chance for you to try out drama and see whether that is one ministry avenue for you."

When holding tryouts, begin by giving the actors a summary of the play. Explain the theme and give a brief description of each character. Provide scripts, or a cutting from a larger script, for each actor. Have actors read for the role they think they would like to perform. Request that they also read for another character if time is available. Have them read for the role of a character of the opposite sex if you want to get a feel for how versatile the actor might be.

What to evaluate at tryouts:

☐▶ Voice—Including projection, control, flexibility, sense of timing, and interpretation.
☐▶ Dramatic personality—Imagination. Is the actor able to convey character?
☐▶ Acting experience—This can be both helpful and harmful. Don't overlook persons with no experience; they could become your best actors.
☐▶ Cooperative attitude—Acting can be taught; desire can't. Is the actor faithful, available, and teachable? How industrious and dependable is he or she? Does he or she get along well with others?

Worship Feast: 15 Sketches for Youth Group, Worship, & More

❏▶ Physical appearance and control—Is he or she physically believable in the role? Will the audience accept your choice visually? Pay attention to what the script requires.

❏▶ The rehearsal schedule—Will the actor be able to commit to attending rehearsals? Find out this information at the tryout. Have each person sign a rehearsal covenant. An example covenant, which may be photocopied, is on page 127.

REHEARSALS

Distribute a rehearsal schedule to all cast members and their parents. Have each actor sign the rehearsal covenant. Actors may be excused only by prior permission from the director. This requirement means that they must have permission from the director to miss a rehearsal; if not, the part will be given to someone else.

Decide where to hold rehearsals. Rehearsing in the actual space in which you will perform is ideal. If not, find a room where you can block out the same space as the stage area. Privacy is a concern. Rehearsals are not open to the public; they are for cast members only. Outsiders should not be allowed at rehearsals unless the director invites them for a specific reason. Rehearsals are a time for trial and error. Trust is needed among cast members to attempt new interpretations. Visitors will put a damper on the creativity of the players.

From the start, set up guidelines for rehearsals. Clearly communicate your expectations. If you expect the group to give the best performance possible, find numerous ways to communicate this. When given a choice between a second-rate and an excellent performance, most groups don't want to bother with a mediocre performance if they can give an exceptional one.

Plays, like seeds, need enough time to germinate.

The director must communicate the importance of rehearsals in accomplishing the group goals. All attention must be on stage. When not on stage, actors may observe the rehearsal and learn from directions given to others; or actors may practice lines in a hallway with another actor or alone. No idle chatter is to be permitted during rehearsals. The first time that cast members who are not on stage talk, gently ask them to be quiet and tell them that the next time they will be asked to leave. The next time, do ask them to leave.

Plays, like seeds, need enough time to germinate. Rehearsals are the soil, water, and light of your productions. Even for a short skit, you will usually need at least one hour for a rehearsal; but you might need only three or four rehearsals. For a longer play, like the one in Chapter 5, you may need to have two-hour rehearsals and have as many as ten to twenty rehearsals. Begin and end rehearsals on time.

TYPICAL REHEARSAL SCHEDULE

The rehearsal schedule begins when you set a date both for the performance and for the first rehearsal. Then you will know how much rehearsal time you have. Starting with the premise that you have very limited time, let's focus on what needs to happen during rehearsals. Before the first rehearsal, you will need to visualize the play; block the play in your mind (or on paper). Blocking is the process of establishing when each actor enters and exits and where each actor stands at every point in the play.

Read through the entire play as a cast. Discuss the meaning of the play, each character, the character's motivations and relationships. Give everyone the rehearsal schedule and emphasis the "off-book" date (the date when all lines are memorized and printed scripts are no longer used).

Run through the entire play, walking through the blocking, with scripts in hand. Be sure that all actors have a pencil to record the blocking notes on their scripts. Blocking also includes all movement—when to turn, sit, and stand—and when to face other actors or the audience.

Rehearse with scripts. For longer plays, divide the play into scenes or sections and rehearse sections separately. Continue to give blocking suggestions at each rehearsal as actors are learning their lines. Blocking reinforces lines and thus assists with memorization. When learning lines, actors should walk through their movement.

Rehearse without scripts. A date by which lines must be memorized (be off-book) was set before the first read through. If you don't insist that the actors meet this deadline, they will never really be weaned from their scripts. Remind them that it is better to miss lines at rehearsals than at a performance. Let the actors struggle. After a while, stop prompting. Do not have a prompter at performances. Concentrate on one of the following at each rehearsal:

Actors must learn to use their bodies as if the audience were deaf, and their voices as if the audience were blind.

- ❏▶ Projection and enunciation
- ❏▶ Characterization
- ❏▶ Believability
- ❏▶ Reason for and use of props and costumes
- ❏▶ Timing

Run lines. Run through the entire play, having actors give their lines without scripts or blocking. Although not all groups use this technique, it can be an effective way to emphasize the impact of the actors' voices. Someone once said that actors must learn to use their bodies as if the audience were deaf, and their voices as if the audience were blind.

DRESS REHEARSAL

It is always prudent to have a dress rehearsal prior to the first performance. A dress rehearsal can help eliminate surprises. Using any prop, costume, sound effects, microphone, lights, or set for the first time can have a serious effect on the performance. Actors need to experience the "feel" of their costumes, how to handle props, and how to work around scenery. The dress rehearsal is a good time to invite a small audience to preview your drama. An audience presence can help the cast learn to hold for laughs. Dress rehearsals should be run as though they were an actual performance. If you plan to give an introduction to the play, read Scripture, play music, or adjust the house lights just prior to the performance, include these in your dress rehearsal. If a curtain call is appropriate at the conclusion of the performance, include this in the dress rehearsal as well. During this rehearsal, the play should be run without any interruptions or corrections.

ACTING TECHNIQUES

Good acting begins with understanding your character. Each actor should read through the script and be able to answer the following questions:

- ▶ Who am I? (includes but is not limited to name, age, personality, and appearance)
- ▶ What time is it? (year, month, day, time)
- ▶ Where am I? (location, room, weather)
- ▶ What is around me? (sights, sounds, smells)
- ▶ What are my relationships? (not only to others in the scene, but my family, school, job, social circles)
- ▶ Who is with me now? (in this scene)
- ▶ What is my objective?
- ▶ What motivates me?
- ▶ What prevents me from getting what I want?
- ▶ What was I doing before the scene began?
- ▶ What will I do after the scene is over?

When actors know who they are and why they are in the play, they can begin to memorize lines with the proper interpretation. Actors must stay in character at all times during the performance. When they are on stage, they must hear the other actors' lines as though it were the first time they have ever heard the lines. They should react as the character would, but they should not overreact. When an actor delivers a line, he or she must deliver it as a part of the ongoing conversation, not as "Oh, it's my turn to deliver a line."

> *When actors know who they are and why they are in the play, they can begin to memorize lines with the proper inflection.*

STAGE DIRECTIONS

A stage—or any performing area—is divided into nine sections. The right and left orientation are from the point of view of the actors while facing the audience. This makes it fairly easy for the actors taking direction but difficult for the director, who is facing the stage and must reverse right and left as directions are given. See page 21.

AUDIENCE

The terms *upstage* and *downstage* come from a time when theaters had seating (and general admission standing) on a flat surface, rather than on the slanted audience seating that we see now in most stadium seating, auditoriums, and sanctuaries. In order for actors in the back part of the stage to be seen, the stage itself was slanted; thus the back of the stage was higher (or up) than the front (down) of the stage. To walk from the front of the stage to the back, actors literally had to walk *up*stage.

These stage directions produced the common phrase "upstaging someone." This means taking the attention away from another and putting it on you. If one actor walks upstage while talking to another actor, the common reaction for the second actor is to turn toward the speaker—thus away from the audience. Because actors always want to keep their faces toward the audience, this maneuver takes the attention away from the actor who had to turn.

By the same token, when you gesture, using your downstage arm, it turns your body away from the audience. As much as possible, always gesture with your upstage arm.

PRACTICAL RULES FOR STAGE DIRECTION

- ❏▶ Use different areas of the stage. Don't play everything downstage center.
- ❏▶ Straight lines and semicircles provide no center of focus.
- ❏▶ Movement changes as thoughts change.
- ❏▶ Create triangular configurations for focus when blocking more than two characters on stage.
- ❏▶ Actors should generally take more than three steps at a time.

SETS, COSTUMES, AND PROPS

An important criterion for most church groups is versatile staging that can take place in any setting. The plays in chapters 3 and 4 are quite simple to stage. They have been executed in churches, in schools, on professional stages before audiences of thousands, and in small rooms in nursing homes for fewer than ten people.

Use minimum costuming and props to create a believable play.

When it comes to staging, use minimum costuming and props to create a believable play. A hat can do as much to suggest character as can an entire costume. Don't begin with elaborate costuming and sets. Think, *What is the minimum costuming and props that will convey in a powerful way the characters, the setting, and the plot?* Groups are often too ambitious. They spend so much time transforming the chancel into a theatre that they don't get around to the essentials of good acting. The audience wants to enter the make-believe of theatre. Good acting is the finest tool to create believable drama.

One time, following a performance at a local metropolitan church, the organizer compared our group to a touring drama company that had been there the month before. "We enjoyed your plays more and your acting was better, but the other group had a whole trunk of costumes and props. You should talk to them to get some ideas." We wondered whether the organizer had ever put the two together? Most groups can improve by concentrating on basic acting skills—not the addition of costumes, sets, and props. When staging, ask; "Is this item absolutely necessary?" Strip away the non-essentials; use only the sets, costumes, and props that are absolutely essential.

Common Acting Problems— Don't Let Them Happen to You!

☐▶ You break character.

☐▶ You are not open to direction.

☐▶ You do not work cooperatively with others. (Prima donnas need not apply!)

☐▶ You do not learn your lines or blocking.

☐▶ You talk too quietly or too fast (due to nervousness).

☐▶ You can't be seen; you allow other actors to block the audience's view of you.

☐▶ You do not deliver lines at the right time; you don't pick up on your cues.

☐▶ You move aimlessly on stage or shift your weight back and forth.

☐▶ You repeat a line when you've missed it or you mouth another actor's lines.

☐▶ You overact or act mechanically.

Stage Directions

Up Right	Up Center	Up Left
Right Center	Center Stage	Left Center
Down Right	Down Center	Down Left

Audience

From WORSHIP FEAST: 15 SKETCHES FOR YOUTH GROUP, WORSHIP, & MORE, by Beth Miller. © 2003 by Abingdon Press.

Practical Rules for Stage Movement

WALKING

- ☐▶ When you walk, start with the upstage foot. This rule keeps you open to the audience.
- ☐▶ Generally, move only on your own line.
- ☐▶ Always cross in front (downstage) of others when giving a line.
- ☐▶ If someone crosses in front of you, counter cross—move in the opposite direction one or two steps. This action keeps you visible to the audience.

STANDING

- ☐▶ Never stand with your back to the audience.
- ☐▶ A profile body position cuts off half of the audience's view; generally a three-quarter out or full-front body position works best.
- ☐▶ The focus of attention is generally on the person speaking; everyone should be looking in the speaker's direction.
- ☐▶ Keep your body still, with your feet firmly planted, and your weight forward on the balls of your feet. Nervous energy often translates into fidgeting and constantly moving feet.

GENERAL

- ☐▶ Gesture with your upstage hand or arm.
- ☐▶ Every movement must be for a purpose, motivated by what your character is thinking, saying, and feeling. Excessive movement detracts; minimal movement emphasizes a change in thought or mood.
- ☐▶ Action should emphasize dialogue and communicate the characters' relationships with one another.
- ☐▶ Never have eye contact with the audience; an actor's visual focus should be on stage or just over the heads of the audience.
- ☐▶ Remember that entrances come from a definite place and that exits go to a definite place. Know where that place is.
- ☐▶ Memorize your movement or blocking in conjunction with your lines.

Chapter 3:
Thematic Sketches

Faith Prints Anonymous

COSTUMES/PROPS REQUIRED: None

CHARACTERS: Six—written as four females and two males, but most of the parts are interchangeable. Change the names to suit your cast. We used the actual names of the persons who toured this play. If you have fewer than six persons, eliminate characters from the group.

SETTING: Faith Prints Anonymous is a weekly meeting of a self-help group for persons who show evidence of the Christian faith. Each character tells of a deeper commitment and development of their faith.

THEME: Living the Christian faith, walking the talk, evangelism

BACKGROUND: This sketch was developed from a skit improvised at our annual youth spring spiritual life retreat. The retreat theme was "Faith Prints." The retreat focused on how we were living our faith. Did our lives truly reflect what we professed? Just as a person leaves fingerprints and footprints, people leave "faith prints" on our lives. In addition to reflecting on those who had left faith imprints on our souls, we challenged ourselves to be intentional about making our own "faith prints."

The "Faith Prints" scripts came together in time for a performance at an invitational youth worship service we sponsored for area churches. The Strangely Warmed Players were preparing new scripts for the International Christian Youth Conference on Evangelism at the University of Ulster. "Faith Prints Anonymous" was well received by the international audience; the message related effectively to many cultures. It fit the bill for that Ireland tour. It was also a call to evangelism, to reflect the gospel through our actions.

DISCUSSION QUESTIONS FOLLOWING THE PERFORMANCE:
☐▶ What were the three "rules" for the group? What did the "rules" symbolize?
☐▶ With which character did you identify? Why?
☐▶ If you most identified with the group facilitator, Nathan, why do you think you did?
☐▶ If you were at the Faith Prints Anonymous support group, what would be your "confession" at this week's meeting?
☐▶ Where have you found a support group that encourages you to grow in your Christian life?

DIRECTOR'S NOTES: It is important to "build" the emotional tone of this sketch. Laura's opening story should not be overly expressive. Each character should say his or her lines with building intensity, until Megan's final speech. She should be sobbing by the time she tells about praying in front of all her friends. The reaction of the group to each story is imperative. In delivering Catriona's line: "I don't just teach Sunday school; I TEACH SUNDAY SCHOOL," each word of the second phrase should be precisely emphasized.

Faith Prints Anonymous

by Beth Miller

NATHAN: Welcome to tonight's meeting of Faith Prints Anonymous, a support group for those who show evidence of the Christian Faith. Let's go over the group rules before we begin. First, what's said in FPA stays in FPA. Second, no put-downs. This is a place of acceptance. No judging others. And third, I know this will be difficult, but we insist—no Bibles. Who wants to go first?

LAURA: Hi, my name is Laura. (*Everyone says, "Hi, Laura."*) I had a really upsetting experience this week. It's difficult to share. I was walking down the hall at school, having a great day. Then I saw this girl who doesn't have any friends. She had dropped her entire armload of books and papers all over the hall. Kids were just walking on top of her stuff. Well, I helped her pick them up. Then I heard someone saying; "Hey, look at Laura! Doing your good deed for the day, Laura?" Do any of you know what it feels like to get caught? (*Several raise their hands.*)

NATHAN: We've all been caught before; every one of us. We know what it feels like. Hang in there, Laura.

AUSTIN: Hi, my name is Austin. (*Everyone says, "Hi, Austin."*) My youth group goes to a nursing home each week to visit with the residents. There's a lot of peer pressure to go. You can't really be part of the group unless you do. I didn't really want to go. I felt uncomfortable at first. I mean, what could I have in common with a ninety-year-old? Well, I have to tell you: I never miss a week now. I know this old guy's stories so well, I can tell them myself. I discovered we have a lot in common. I even know the difference between B-5 and G-58 in Bingo.

NATHAN: It's really amazing where this can lead you—places you would never picture yourself going. We've all been there, Austin.

JO: Hi, my name is Jo. (*Everyone says, "Hi, Jo."*) It all started for me about six months ago. This really good friend, someone I really admired and trusted, invited me to go to a Bible study with her. At first, I remembered what my teachers and parents taught me. So I just said, "No!" Then I told her that I just wasn't interested. Then I made up excuses for why I couldn't go. Well, eventually she got to me. She was so persistent. She wouldn't let up, and I, I . . . I caved. I went. I've been going to Bible study every week since. I can't stop. Bible study has become an important part of my life.

From WORSHIP FEAST: 15 SKETCHES FOR YOUTH GROUP, WORSHIP, & MORE, by Beth Miller. © 2003 by Abingdon Press.

NATHAN: It's hard to stop, Jo; it's addictive. We understand. One day at a time.

NATHAN: I'd like for you all to welcome a new member tonight. Everyone, this is Catriona.

CATRIONA: Hi, my name is Catriona. (*Everyone says, "Hi Catriona."*) It began innocently enough. I mean, I was brought up in the church. I was baptized, confirmed—all the usual stuff. I went to Sunday school and youth group. I suppose it was a gradual thing; but one day, I realized that I should teach Sunday school. It's not like I just teach Sunday school, I mean I TEACH SUNDAY SCHOOL. It's been going on now for two years. I study my lesson plan and read the Bible background material, I pray for each member of the class, I write notes if they miss a Sunday, and I send them birthday cards. I love singing the Jesus songs with these little kids. Craft time is exhilarating for me. It's a real high— and we're not sniffing the glue! I realized one day that I really cared about these kids. I mean, I really love them—unconditionally. (*She starts to cry.*) I'm sorry. I'm afraid that I'll be doing this for years. I don't think I can stop.

LAURA: (*To the group*) Group hug. (*Everyone does a group hug.*)
(*To Catriona*) Hugs are therapy.

NATHAN: Megan, looks like you're last. Want to wrap it up for tonight?

MEGAN: Hi, my name is Megan. (*Everyone says, "Hi Megan."*) OK, this is hard. I don't like to talk about it, but maybe my story will help someone else. I can't stop praying! I pray all the time. The other day I was at an amusement park with my friends. We were on the roller coaster—at the top. I used to be able to just clench my fists, close my eyes, and scream. But this time, I started praying—OUT LOUD! In front of my friends! (*She's sobbing by now. Everyone else looks shocked.*) And the worst part is, now I pray even when I'm not afraid!

LAURA: (*Said under her breath. She gets a reprimanding look from Nathan.*) Freak! Whew, and I thought I was bad.

NATHAN: Excuse me, Laura? Thank you all for sharing tonight. We appreciate your honesty. It came from the heart. Remember that change doesn't happen overnight—it takes a lifetime. But it happens with each step we take, one step at a time. Let's repeat our prayer together:

EVERYONE: Lord, grant me the serenity to accept the things I cannot change, the courage to change the things I can, and the wisdom to know the difference.

FROM WORSHIP FEAST: 15 SKETCHES FOR YOUTH GROUP, WORSHIP, & MORE, by Beth Miller. © 2003 by Abingdon Press.

MacJesus to Go

COSTUMES/PROPS REQUIRED: We sewed a gold letter *M* on a blue shirt for the Cashier. The nuns used several yards of black cotton fabric held around their faces to look like habits. The other actors suggested their characters with hats.

CHARACTERS: Seven. If you don't have enough actors, cut one of the scenes

SETTING: a fast-food restaurant, serving the brand of Christianity or religion you choose

THEME: Salvation. Do we choose to follow Jesus, or would we rather choose the "jesus" we would like to follow?

BACKGROUND: Jon wrote the original version of this sketch in 1999 for our youth worship service. It has become the trademark piece for the Strangely Warmed Players. Each new troupe makes revisions, contributes new characters for development and comes up with new lines. Following a performance before the World Methodist Conference, a delegate from Belgium asked if he could translate it into French and use it to teach evangelism in his seminary class. Unfortunately, because of the global nature of American fast-food, the concept of a MacJesus is understood by almost every culture. We've had requests from Africa University and a church in Estonia to use this play.

Catriona and Megan Jo decided to do their characters as nuns on our Northern Ireland tour. This was a bit risky, but it worked. They hadn't brought costumes, so they improvised habits with sheets from their dorm rooms. Megan's favorite character from *Saturday Night Live* is the "joy-ologist." She improvised her part based on this character. Her lines came out of this improv session.

DISCUSSION QUESTIONS FOLLOWING THE PERFORMANCE:
❑▶ What made you laugh? Why?
❑▶ With which character did you identify? Why?
❑▶ What was the symbolism of the "I can handle only for Christmas and Easter" line?
❑▶ What were the nuns hoping to find?
❑▶ Have you ever known persons who will seek whatever is spiritually popular?
❑▶ What was the Happy Meal customer seeking?
❑▶ What line really surprised you? Why?
❑▶ How do we alter Christ's message to suit our needs?
❑▶ What spiritual truth or insight did you gain from this play?

DIRECTOR'S NOTES: Establish two locations—one for the Cashier and another spot where the other character's order. We usually locate these a few feet apart. The Cashier must never look at the customers, and the customers must never look at the Cashier. Lines are given directly to the audience, remembering never to have eye contact with the audience but to focus above their heads at a spot on the far wall. All of the customers should use exactly the same spot to place their orders.

MacJesus to Go

by Jon Stroud and Beth Miller

CASHIER: Welcome to MacJesus to Go—more salvation for your money. May I take your order, please.

AUSTIN: Yeah, I'm really in a bit of a rush—nothing too heavy.

CASHIER: We've got a 5-piece prayer MacNugget with Sweet and Simple sauce. Super-size it, and we'll throw in a "going to heaven" money-back guarantee!

AUSTIN: Um, that's a little too much. . . . I need something on the run.

CASHIER: How about the 4-piece Holiday Onion Rings, complete with Christmas, Palm Sunday, Easter, and Pentecost?

AUSTIN: Whoa, no way, man. I can handle only Christmas and Easter. That's all I really have time for. But I do want a Shake of Self-righteousness to wash it all down.

CASHIER: All right, sir. That'll cost you . . . church membership and joining the church softball team—nothing you can't afford.

AUSTIN: Thanks, but make it fast. I've got a football game to get to.

CASHIER: All right, please move to the next window. (*Austin exits. Catriona and Megan Jo come up to the window.*) Hello, and welcome to MacJesus to Go—it's your way, right away at MacJesus now. May I take your order?

CATRIONA: All right, this is a BIG order. We're serious. . . . I want one of those double-decker, triple-pounder Rich Young Ruler burgers.

MEGAN JO: I want the Good Samaritan sandwich—with everything on it.

CASHIER: Extra preachy?

CATRIONA: You bet your bippy, Mister.

MEGAN JO: I want Forgiveness Fries, a Sanctified Shake . . . and throw in some of those Sinless Cinnamon Thingies . . .

CATRIONA: And I want ALL the sauces, the Sweet and Simple, the Holiness Honey, and two packets of the Blue Cheeses of Nazareth!

CASHIER: Just let me ring that up here. (*He pretends to ring in the order.*) All right, that'll be a lifetime of over-zealousness, going the extra mile, lending a helping hand, and having a "holier than thou" attitude!

CATRIONA: (*She and Megan Jo nod eagerly to each other.*) All right.

MEGAN JO: Sounds good. (*She and Catriona exit. Laura comes up to the window.*)

CASHIER: Welcome to MacJesus to Go. We do Jesus right. Here at MacJesus to Go, our Jesus is finger-lickin' good. May I take your order, please?

LAURA: I just want whatever is selling. What's popular? Like if Britney Spears was here, what would she order?

CASHIER: There's the Kentucky-fried Jesus. You'd hardly even recognize that it's Jesus at all. . . .

LAURA: That's perfect! How much?

CASHIER: Offer prayers once a week to the deity of your choice, seek serenity, share concern, live totally.

LAURA: Thanks! This is too good to be true! (*Laura exits. Megan comes up to the window.*)

CASHIER: Welcome to MacJesus to go. Why not try our Salvation salad with Hidden Valley of Death ranch dressing? And if you get it with the value meal, you get extra serenity and blessed assurance.

MEGAN: I just love sunshine and trees and rainbows and butterflies.

CASHIER: Could I interest you in a Happy Meal Jesus. It has a little Jesus and a whole lot more?

MEGAN: That's wonderful! It makes me joyful right down to the tips of my toes. I want to get real spiritual. See these crystals. (*Holds out hand as if showing crystals.*) I'm a spiritual lady. Does this Happy Meal come with any merry little icons, any idols?

CASHIER: Well, you have your choice of Santa Claus, the Easter Bunny, or a St. Patrick's Day leprechaun.

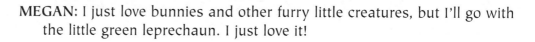

MEGAN: I just love bunnies and other furry little creatures, but I'll go with the little green leprechaun. I just love it!

CASHIER: Anything else we can add to your joy?

MEGAN: Definitely a McFluffy treat with little joy sprinkles.

CASHIER: All right, a Happy Meal with the leprechaun and a McFluffy treat. That will cost you your soul.

MEGAN: That'll be great! Thanks! (*Megan exits. Nathan comes to the window.*)

CASHIER: Yo Quiero Jesus Christ. Welcome to MacJesus to go. May I take your order, please?

NATHAN: Yes, hello. I'd like the plain Jesus, if its not too much trouble.

CASHIER: All right. Is that going to be an extra-value meal? Super-sized?

NATHAN: No. I don't think you understand. I just want the plain Jesus, the original.

CASHIER: Would that be with or without Forgiveness Fries? Ketchup? Mustard? With Charity Cheese? Do you want the Extra-Preachy Jesus?

NATHAN: Please, I just want Jesus. I don't need any of the extras—just the Jesus who died on the cross.

CASHIER: Ohhh . . . sorry, Dude. I think we discontinued that Jesus.

NATHAN: Oh?

CASHIER: Yeah, he didn't sell so well. (*Nathan shakes his head and turns away, walks slowly with head down.*) That reminds me of a song. . . . (*Sings.*) Do you believe in Jesus? And I hope you do. He's the savior, and he died on the cross. . . . (*Stops singing.*) That doesn't rhyme—won't ever sell. Oh well. Welcome to MacJesus to Go. May I take your order, please?

Teach Me to Pray

COSTUMES/PROPS REQUIRED: None

CHARACTERS: This play can be staged with as few as four actors playing various parts. However, it will accommodate as many as twelve actors.

SETTING: "Teach Me to Pray" is a series of seven prayer vignettes.

THEME: Most of us need to learn from Christ how to pray—what prayer is really about. These vignettes depict what prayer is not.

BACKGROUND: This sketch was written for our fall youth retreat on prayer. Each scene was written to challenge our ideas and patterns for prayer. We knew that learning what something is not can be as enlightening as describing what something actually is. Laughter can be a powerful agent for insight and change.

The first official performance of this sketch was for the National Board of Pension Officers of the United Methodist Church. The Strangely Warmed Players were to provide entertainment, following the evening meal.

One of the vignettes was included in *Surviving Life's Jungle* (Abingdon Press's Faith in Motion junior high curriculum). At a Sunday night youth program entitled "Oh, God: How Do We Use the Lord's Name?" the topic was introduced by a portrayal of the third scene of the teen crush. This sketch is versatile and easy to perform.

DISCUSSION QUESTIONS FOLLOWING THE PERFORMANCE:
❑▶ What made you laugh? Why?
❑▶ With which prayer did you most identify? Why?
❑▶ What was the first woman attempting to do in her prayer?
❑▶ What was the point of the prayer over dinner?
❑▶ Does God take sides?
❑▶ Which of these prayers requested God to do something against God's character?
❑▶ Can prayer change the nature of God? Does prayer change our nature?
❑▶ How did people try to bargain with God in the prayers?
❑▶ Why is the last line of the play so powerful?
❑▶ Do we ever just say prayers and not mean them? Why?

DIRECTOR'S NOTES: Timing is extremely important in this sketch. The entire cast should take the stage at the beginning. If you are casting every part (twelve characters), consider posing everyone on the stage, frozen before and after their own vignette. Another option is for the entire cast to stand frozen with their backs to the audience in a group at the back of the stage. Each of them should then turn and come quickly forward to do his or her individual scene. There should be only a single beat between scenes. (Of course, hold for laughter.)

Teach Me to Pray

by Beth Miller

EMMA: Bet you can't stick this crayon up your nose!

ROGER: Bet you can't eat this worm.

KIMMI: Hey, Rob, bet you won't kiss Emma.

ROB: I've got one. Bet none of you can say the Lord's Prayer.

ROGER: I can do that. Now I lay me down to sleep. I pray the Lord my soul to keep. If I should die before I wake, I pray the Lord my soul to take.

ROGER: Pay up.

ROB: Aw shucks! Here.

KIMMI: Wow, Roger, I didn't know you were so spiritual!

PRAYER 2

MOTHER: It's time for supper, would someone please offer grace?

DAUGHTER: We got bread and we got meat, why the dickens don't we eat?

SON: Rub a dub dub, thanks for the grub. Yeah, God!

MOTHER: Would someone please offer a serious prayer?

FATHER: Oh almighty oneness, we beseech thee, lookest down uponst us and grant unto us, hitherto unbeknownst erstwhile unto thee, thy humble children, thankfulness of being for what hast been bestowed uponst us for four score and seven years, brought forth on this continent as a new consideration, when the force was with us, before E.T. phoned home, with liberty and justice for all.

EVERYONE: Amen! (*The children look a bit puzzled.*)

MOTHER: Thank you.

PRAYER 3

TEENAGE GIRL: OK, God. Like, I have this HUGE crush on Drew; and he, like, never seems to notice me. And then today at lunch, I dropped my tray, like, right in front of him, in front of the whole school. Like, oh, my God! Oops, sorry! Well, he was, like, so nice and helped me pick up the mess; and he, like, notices me! I'm about to drop dead—really, I'm not, like, ready to die or anything. It's just a figure of speech, so don't get any ideas. Well along comes Jennifer; and she, like, tosses her hair and bats her eyelashes at Drew. And he, like, asks her out to the football game Friday night. Like—oh, my God! Sorry, did it again—right in front of me! So I was thinkin' . . . since you're on my side and all, couldn't you just, like, break her leg? (*Long pause.*) Maybe if that's, like, too drastic, just make sure she has a bad hair day! That would be great!

PRAYER 4

TEENAGE BOY: Dear God, I really need the car Saturday night. If I could have the car Saturday night, I'll go to Sunday school and youth group. I'll even attend church. You see, Catriona finally said yes! I have a date with Catriona Saturday night. . . . So if I could have the car, I will . . . dedicate my life to your service. I'll . . . go to seminary and become a minister. I just have to have the car. I'll be a missionary to the natives of Bongo Bongo and live in abject poverty. Really, this means so much to me. If you could just convince my parents to loan me the car . . . I'll do ANYTHING! Thank you, Lord. Amen.

TEENAGE BOY: Dad, may I have the car Saturday night?

FATHER: Sure, just remember that we expect you to get up and go to church with us Sunday morning.

TEENAGE BOY: Why can't you just give me the car? Why do you always have to bargain with me?

PRAYER 5

OLDER WOMAN: Oh God, you are well aware of my work for you. I am your dedicated servant. I attend church faithfully every Sunday. I have served as the women's president for fifteen years. I chaired the all-church rummage sale three years in a row. I serve meals to the homeless. I have filled countless missionary barrels with old clothing, cancelled stamps, and used tea bags. I taught junior high Sunday school for twenty-eight years! So please let me win the lottery. Amen.

PRAYER 6

TEENAGE BOY: OK, guys, let's pray! God, this is a really big game.

TEAMMATES: Yes.

TEENAGE BOY: Brother Andrew's is a better team. They're a bigger team. I mean, look at those guys! It's David and Goliath all over again. We know that you are often on the side of the underdog. Well . . . Underdogs R Us!

TEAMMATES: Yes.

TEENAGE BOY: So, God, you are on our side!

TEAMMATES: Yes.

TEENAGE BOY: Let's face it! We always lose to them, so we figure it's our turn to win. That's only fair, you know. So help us wipe them out.

TEAMMATES: (*Louder.*) Yes.

TEENAGE BOY: Help us smash them into oblivion!

TEAMMATES: (*Shouting.*) Yes.

TEENAGE BOY: Let's hurt someone!

TEAMMATES: (*Yelling.*) Yes.

TEENAGE BOY: Help us annihilate them!

TEAMMATES: (*Screaming.*) Yes.

TEENAGE BOY: (*Softly.*) Shhhh! In Jesus' name, amen.

PRAYER 7

YOUNG GIRL: (*Said very slowly*) Now I lay me down to sleeeeeeeeeeeeeeep.

MOTHER: It's late. Could you, please, hurry a bit?

YOUNG GIRL: I pray the Loooooord, my soul to keeeeeeeeeeeeeeeep.

MOTHER: Anna, you are stalling. Get on with the prayer

YOUNG GIRL: If I should diiiiiiiiiiiiiiie, before. . . . AM I GOING TO DIE?

MOTHER: No, you are not going to die. Finish the prayer.

YOUNG GIRL: If I should die, before I wake . . . ARE YOU SURE I'M NOT GOING TO DIE BEFORE I WAKE?

MOTHER: Just finish the prayer, and go to sleep. *E.R.* is on in ten minutes.

YOUNG GIRL: (*Almost crying, definitely scared.*) If I should die before I wake, I pray the Lord my soul to take. I'M GOING TO DIE, AND SOMEONE IS GOING TO TAKE MY SOUL! I DON'T WANT TO LOSE MY SOUL!

MOTHER: Will you calm down. Anna. You are not going to die, and you are not going to lose your soul. Now GO TO SLEEP!

YOUNG GIRL: If I'm not going to die and I'm not going to lose my soul, then why do we pray that?

MOTHER: We don't really mean it. We just say it because it's part of the prayer.

The Witness Protection Program

COSTUMES/PROPS REQUIRED: Disguise for Saul (It could be sunglasses or one of those funny nose, moustache, glasses combinations.)

CHARACTERS: Two. They can be one male and one female or the same sex (just change the names).

SETTING: The waiting room for God's witness protection program

THEME: Transformation, grace, faith

BACKGROUND: This sketch was written for Youth '03, a global gathering of United Methodist youth. Their theme was "Reach: Higher, Deeper, Further." "Witness Protection Program" focuses on two persons waiting to make a decision about allowing God to change them. The process requires the leap of faith that takes us higher, deeper, further. This play symbolizes that first step toward transformation. It plays off the government's witness protection program.

The names were chosen to connect with Paul's story in the New Testament and Sarah's story in the Old Testament. Both of these characters opened themselves up to God's changing power. The play is purposely vague about where they go from this room and what happens next. A number of interpretations work.

DISCUSSION QUESTIONS FOLLOWING THE PERFORMANCE:
❏▶ What images do you think of when you hear "witness protection program"?
❏▶ With which character did you identify, Why?
❏▶ What do you think brought each character to this room?
❏▶ One character wanted a nose job. What would be first on your list of desired changes?
❏▶ How are you comfortable with "the old me"?
❏▶ What does being changed "from the inside out" mean to you?
❏▶ What brings people to the point of transformation?
❏▶ What is scary about transformation?
❏▶ What made you laugh? Why?
❏▶ What line really surprised you? Why?
❏▶ What spiritual truth or insight did you gain from this play?

DIRECTOR'S NOTES: When blocking this play, listen carefully to what lines draw the characters closer together and what lines pull them away from each other. Use movement to reinforce change of thought.

The Witness Protection Program

by Beth Miller

SAUL: Whoa, I'm not sure I got the right room?

SARAH: Witness Protection Program?

SAUL: Yea.

SARAH: Right place. Nervous?

SAUL: A little. Aren't you?

SARAH: Sure. (*Pause.*) I don't think that you'll need the disguise anymore.

SAUL: Really? (*Removes glasses, mustache. Looks around cautiously.*) I done some pretty bad things. These guys are after me. This guy says he's gonna save me from all that. Sure hope I can trust him.

SARAH: You grew up in the Bronx?

SAUL: It shows, don't it? Ya suppose they can do something about the accent?

SARAH: I'm not sure.

SAUL: What about the nose? I was kinda hopin' I could get a nose job out of it.

SARAH: I think that this is more about changing what's on the inside—not external appearances.

SAUL: I was afraid of that.

SAUL: (*Pause.*) Ever known anyone who has gone through the program before?

SARAH: My parents.

SAUL: Really? (*Shows genuine interest.*) Wow. Yer parents! What was it like for 'em?

From WORSHIP FEAST: 15 SKETCHES FOR YOUTH GROUP, WORSHIP, & MORE, by Beth Miller. © 2003 by Abingdon Press.

SARAH: Changed their lives.

SAUL: That's what I was afraid of!

SARAH: Haven't you known anyone?

SAUL: Not really. I mean, not personally. I heard about people; I seen stories on the TV. . . .

SARAH: My parents say it was the best thing that ever happened to them.

SAUL: Is that why you're here?

SARAH: Partly, but also because it's my choice. What about you?

SAUL: I'm not really sure why I'm here. Feelin' a little like I was "chosen."

SARAH: We all are . . . "chosen." But, you know, they can't force it on you. You have to be willing.

SAUL: I know. But I've gotten pretty comfortable with the "old" me.

SARAH: I'm ready for a change.

SAUL: Ya don't seem like the kind a person who needs to change.

SARAH: Appearances aren't everything. So are you ready?

SAUL: Guess so. I'm here.

SARAH: Good, that's the first step.

SAUL: Step? It seems more like a "leap."

SARAH: You're right, it is. Afraid?

SAUL: Hey, I ain't 'fraid of nuttin'. I gotta reputation!

SARAH: Not for long.

SAUL: What's that supposed to mean?

SARAH: Your reputation. You don't have to deal with it anymore. You get a fresh start. You understand? You're given a new identity, a new name.

SAUL: It's still a risk.

From Worship Feast: 15 Sketches for Youth Group, Worship, & More, by Beth Miller. © 2003 by Abingdon Press.

SARAH: But there are trade-offs. You understand that you're given a new identity, a new name?

SAUL: Da "new" me in exchange for da "old" me. I'm not sure I know what I did to deserve this.

SARAH: Maybe that's critical.

VOICE OFF STAGE: Next.

SARAH: Sorry, I've got to go. (*Starts to leave*)

SAUL: Nice talkin' to ya. I'm Saul. Sorry, didn't catch yer name?

SARAH: Sarah. (*Laughs.*) Guess it doesn't really matter. That's all about to change. Welcome to the Witness Protection Program. You are going to go through with it, aren't you?

SAUL: Maybe. Never knew God had a program like this!

Seek and Find

COSTUMES/PROPS REQUIRED: Doughnut box or snack food bag. Do not use actual food; this should be mimed. The box could also be mimed.

CHARACTERS: Two. They can be same sex or one male and one female; however, the discussion questions below are written as if Speaker 1 is male and Speaker 2 is female.

SETTING: Bench outside a bus stop

THEME: Salvation, prevenient and justifying grace.

BACKGROUND: The Strangely Warmed Players were struggling with developing skits on evangelism for an international youth conference on this topic. Door-to-door evangelism is commendable but not something that was part of our tradition. Most of the group's images of evangelism were of a street corner evangelist handing out gospel tracks or of TV evangelists. The Director of World Methodist Evangelism suggested that we read George Hunter's *The Celtic Way of Evangelism: How Christianity Can Reach the West . . . Again,* by George G. Hunter, III. I ordered copies for each cast member.

While discussing the book, the group began to get excited and inspired about evangelism. We realized that many of our scripts—"Teach Me to Pray," "Faith Prints Anonymous," and "Survivor"—portrayed concepts from Dr. Hunter's book. Evangelism should be natural and should flow from living your faith. Sharing faith should be easy and sincere. Faith sharing is most powerful when offered after we have already developed a relationship with another person. "Seek and Find" was written for the International Christian Youth Conference in Belfast, Ireland, in 2002. It was included, along with "Faith Prints Anonymous" and "Teach Me to Pray," in *Worship Feast: Services* (Abingdon Press, 2003).

DISCUSSION QUESTIONS FOLLOWING THE PERFORMANCE:
- ▶ What did Speaker 1 mean when he indicated that he was hungry?
- ▶ What was the first reaction of Speaker 1 to Speaker 2's request to fill her inner hunger?
- ▶ When have you felt uncomfortable about sharing your faith?
- ▶ Speaker 2 is offered truth and responds with "Yours?" What does this mean?
- ▶ What do you think helps Speaker 2 decide to agree?
- ▶ Is finding faith as simple as asking?
- ▶ Reread the play and fill in the rest of the words to make complete sentences. What would you say?

DIRECTOR'S NOTES: Good actors recognize the power of every word. Much of this script is only one word per line. The actors preparing "Seek and Find" must be able to interpret each word with intensity and believability. Pauses need to be used with care and should be well timed. This play requires intense concentration.

Seek and Find

by Beth Miller

(*Two strangers are sitting on a park bench.*)

SPEAKER 1: Nice day.

SPEAKER 2: (*Incredulous*) What?

SPEAKER 1: Nice day.

SPEAKER 2: Not really.

SPEAKER 1: No?

SPEAKER 2: No.

SPEAKER 1: Hungry?

SPEAKER 2: No thanks.

SPEAKER 1: You sure?

SPEAKER 2: Well. . . .

SPEAKER 1: (*Mimes sharing snack food.*) Here.

SPEAKER 2: (*Points to heart.*) No, here.

SPEAKER 1: (*Taken aback.*) Oh!

SPEAKER 2: Well?

SPEAKER 1: (*Unsure.*) Well . . . ah. . . .

SPEAKER 2: Never mind.

SPEAKER 1: No, wait!

SPEAKER 2: Why?

SPEAKER 1: Truth?

SPEAKER 2: Yours?

SPEAKER 1: No. (*Pauses. Tries again.*) Hope?

SPEAKER 2: (*Sarcastically.*) Right!

SPEAKER 1: Love!

SPEAKER 2: Whose?

SPEAKER 1: (*Points upward.*) His.

SPEAKER 2: How?

SPEAKER 1: Ask.

SPEAKER 2: For?

SPEAKER 1: Forgiveness.

SPEAKER 2: Find?

SPEAKER 1: Grace.

SPEAKER 2: Receive?

SPEAKER 1: Life!

SPEAKER 2: Too easy.

SPEAKER 1: Yeah!

SPEAKER 2: No way.

SPEAKER 1: Way. (*Pauses.*) Truth. . . . Life.

SPEAKER 2: You're sure?

SPEAKER 1: Yep.

SPEAKER 2: (*Long pause.*) OK. (*Softly nods as if slowly accepting.*) OK. OK!

SPEAKER 1: OK?

SPEAKER 2: Yeah!

SPEAKER 1: Nice day.

SPEAKER 2: (*Pauses.*) Great day!

Survivor

COSTUMES/PROPS REQUIRED: You may wish to have an item that symbolizes immunity. We originally used a tiki torch. Suggestive costumes are fun to indicate that they are on a tropical island. The Elizabeth character found a fake hair insert that she could pull out on the appropriate line.

CHARACTERS: Seven: one Negotiator/TV Host and six participants going for the challenge of being the survivor. All characters can be either sex. Simply change the names to suit the actors you have. If you don't have enough actors, combine two characters or cut one of the character's lines.

SETTING: A tropical island, a reality TV series

THEME: Grace, forgiveness

BACKGROUND: Megan Jo wrote this sketch for our annual youth worship service. Our theme that year was "Amazing Grace." This was the year the popular television series *Survivor* made its debut. "Survivor" is included in *Surviving Life's Jungle* (Abingdon Press's Faith in Motion junior high curriculum).

At the International Christian Youth Conference in Ireland, we were asked to perform additional plays. fortunately, Megan Jo had brought her script along. An additional character was added to make it an ensemble piece for the seven actors in that particular troupe. We rewrote it one morning, rehearsed the new version that afternoon, and performed it that evening. Note references specific to Ireland. Change these to fit your setting.

DISCUSSION QUESTIONS FOLLOWING THE PERFORMANCE:
❑▶ What made you laugh? Why?
❑▶ With which character did you identify? Why?
❑▶ What line really surprised you? Why?
❑▶ What spiritual truth or insight did you gain from this play?

DIRECTOR'S NOTES: Have fun with the characters in this delightful piece. We made them larger than life, exaggerating their behavior and emotions. The cast had fun putting suggestive costumes together from what they packed in their suitcases.

Survivor

by Megan Jo Crumm

LENNY: (*Biting nails, looking nervous*) I know I'm gonna get voted off.

AUSTIN: Well, maybe if you hadn't burned up our campsite.

LENNY: Hey, it wasn't entirely my fault!

ALICIA: (*Sarcastically.*) Yeah, how were you supposed to know that sparks ignite (*insert your state*) state flags?

LENNY: (*Unaware of the sarcasm*) Exactly! I mean, they don't teach you that stuff in prep school.

KIMMI: (*Starts scratching*) Even you had to know that fire ants aren't seasoning for chili!

LENNY: I never claimed to be a chef!

ELIZABETH: (*Trying to be nice*) Well, maybe he thought they'd be like Cajun peppers?

LENNY: I thought that they would spice it up a bit. Like the Spice Girls.

ALL GIRLS: (*Sings.*) "If you want to be my lover . . ."

LENNY: Aren't they Irish?

AUSTIN: No, they're British!

LENNY: (*Pronounce this "tuh-MAY-toh, tuh-MAH-toh."*) Tomato, tomato!

AUSTIN: Who cares about the Spice Girls? I just wanted my share of the rice!

KIMMI: Yeah, Lenny, you hogged it all!

CANDY: Lenny is a loser.

LENNY: I needed that rice. I was feeling rather anemic.

From WORSHIP FEAST: 15 SKETCHES FOR YOUTH GROUP, WORSHIP, & MORE, by Beth Miller. © 2003 by Abingdon Press.

ELIZABETH: Anemic? My hair is falling out!

ALICIA: (*Yawning*) All I know is I want some sleep. Your bagpipe practice has been keeping me up all night.

CANDY: Lenny is a loser.

LENNY: I promised my mom I'd practice for the Celtic festival.

AUSTIN: How do you get by on so little sleep, anyway?

ALICIA: Does it really matter? Let's just vote him off.

KIMMI: I'd defend you, Lenny; (*shows Lenny her arm*) but look at these bites!

LENNY: It's OK. I guess I'm not a sole survivor.

ALICIA: We could give him a break. But "The Rocky Road to Dublin" all night long? Give me a break!

CANDY: Lenny is a loser.

KIMMI: (*Jeff enters.*) Now we'll find out who gets immunity.

JEFF: Lenny, you look nervous. You've had such a rough time. But you've tried to be a pretty good guy.

LENNY: The piranhas in the drinking water were an honest mistake. Really!

CANDY: Lenny is a loser.

JEFF: Well, now it's time for tribal council. Before the votes, let's reflect on the past three days since our last tribal council. So, Elizabeth, you're first. How do you feel?

ELIZABETH: How do I feel? I'm starving. . . . Lenny hogged all the rice, I'm emaciated, my hair is falling out! How do I feel?

JEFF: Alicia, your time . . . How have things been going the past three days? Alicia, wake up, it's your turn to speak.

ALICIA: Huh? (*Yawns.*) I haven't had more than ten minutes of uninterrupted sleep. You see, a certain someone has been continuously playing "The Rocky Road to Dublin" on his bagpipes. . . . How about sending a certain someone on the rocky road to Dublin and off this island?

JEFF: Kimmi, if you could stop scratching for a minute, it's your turn. How has the group been doing the past three days?

KIMMI: FIRE ANTS! FIRE ANTS in our chili! Lenny is trying to kill all of us!

AUSTIN: He ate all the rice and then ruined our chili with fire ants. Seasoning for chili? What a lame excuse! Talk about lame excuses for a human being.

CANDY: Lenny is a loser.

JEFF: OK, Lenny, it's your turn.

LENNY: I know I'm probably the one who will get voted off tonight—after all the stupid things I've done. But this has been a meaningful experience; it has really changed my life!

JEFF: I know this may sound crazy, but you get the immunity today.

LENNY: (*Stammering*) What? I don't deserve this. I . . . it . . . just. . . .

JEFF: In fact, no one is getting voted off today.

ALL SURVIVORS: What? Huh? How can you do that?

ALICIA: We were all set to get rid of Lenny.

KIMMI: Yeah! We don't deserve this!

JEFF: That's the point. Nobody "deserves" grace.

ELIZABETH: You can't just give him immunity.

JEFF: Sure I can. In fact, I just gave it to everyone. You just have to accept it.

From WORSHIP FEAST: 15 SKETCHES FOR YOUTH GROUP, WORSHIP, & MORE, by Beth Miller. © 2003 by Abingdon Press.

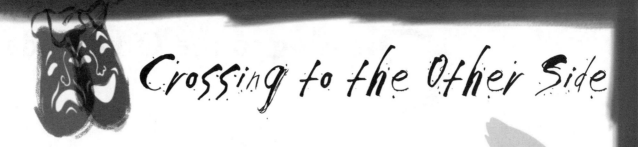

Crossing to the Other Side

COSTUMES/PROPS REQUIRED: Three life preservers, children's floaties, or inflatable rings; pirate bandannas; plastic fish

CHARACTERS: Five. All characters can be either sex.

SETTING: On board a sailboat moored to a dock

THEME: Faith, change, following the Spirit, Luke 8:22

BACKGROUND: This sketch was written for Youth 2003, a global gathering of United Methodist youth. Their theme was "Reach: Higher, Deeper, Further." It was inspired by a sermon by Grace Imathiu at the International Christian Youth Conference in Belfast, in Summer 2002. The title of the play is the title of her sermon based on Luke 8:22.

The original script did not have pirates. The addition of the pirates came out of group rehearsals; the pirates added a twist and humor. The obvious allegory for the boat is a church that is unwilling to follow where the spirit leads, to take risks and change. But the boat could also represent individuals, organizations, or structures unwilling to change. You could use this play for any number of occasions. If you have your own theme for your event, insert it into the final motto quoted by the crew.

DISCUSSION QUESTIONS FOLLOWING THE PERFORMANCE:
❑▶ What made you laugh? Why?
❑▶ With which character did you identify? Why?
❑▶ The Captain's motto is "Safety first." What would be your life motto?
❑▶ Of what is the Captain afraid?
❑▶ Why did the crew come on board?
❑▶ What did the wind symbolize?
❑▶ When have you heard, "We've always done it this way"?
❑▶ What line really surprised you? Why?
❑▶ What spiritual truth or insight did you gain from this play?

DIRECTOR'S NOTES: Establish for the actors the perimeters of the boat. They need to know where the bow, stern, and gangplank are. The crew will mime weighing the anchor, hoisting the main sail, and cutting the dock lines. These details should be rehearsed.

If your actors are comfortable singing, consider an operatic style for "In matters theological, he's the very model of a modern major general" (Gilbert and Sullivan's "The Pirates of Penzance").

If your group is performing this for a small group, you might want to get a poster called RISK from successories.com (item 734142). The tagline on the poster is "A ship in a harbor is safe . . . but that's not what ships were made for."

Crossing to the Other Side

by Beth Miller

CAPTAIN: Welcome aboard, mates!

FIRST MATE: Looks like a great day for sailing.

CREW: I brought the life preservers.

CAPTAIN: Good. You know my motto. . . .

FIRST MATE AND CREW: Wash behind your ears?

CAPTAIN: No! Safety first! Let's go over everything before we get started. If anyone falls overboard, the First Mate throws the man, I mean, person overboard a line. The crew keeps their eyes on the lost person at all times while I circle the boat to recover the person from the depths.

CREW: Not meaning to be rude, Captain, but there are only three of us on board.

CAPTAIN: The *Roget's Complete Annotated Handbook for Water Safety, Volume Seven,* strictly states that we follow this procedure.

FIRST MATE: Remember, Captain, you won't really turn the boat because we will still be tied to the dock.

CAPTAIN: We must do things by the book. Our first concern is saving the lost. And remember our motto. . . .

CREW: One for all, and all for one?

CAPTAIN: No, no, no! Safety first!

CREW: If we never leave the dock, how will we ever save someone who is lost?

CAPTAIN: I run a tight ship, and we will observe correct protocol. Besides, the lost will come to us. (*Pause.*) First, put on your life preservers.

FIRST MATE: Aye, aye, Captain. (*They put on the life preservers.*)

CREW: Not much wind today, sir.

CAPTAIN: Don't worry about wind. We're much safer without it, and you know my motto. . . .

FIRST MATE AND CREW: Be all you can be in the . . .

CAPTAIN: (*Interrupting*) Safety first!

FIRST MATE: There's seems to be strong wind farther out. Perhaps we could untie the lines and actually sail the boat?

CAPTAIN: This boat has never been untied. Why should we start now? Sailing is risky. You never know where the wind will take you. You're much safer at the dock. And you know my motto. . . .

CREW: (*Fabio voice*) I can't believe its not butter?

CAPTAIN: Safety first!

FIRST MATE: I have noticed a boat or two actually sail away from the dock, out into the deeper water.

CAPTAIN: I suppose that if everyone sailed from the dock, you'd sail from the dock? You're a follower. That's why you are the First Mate, and I'm the very model of a modern major general.

FIRST MATE AND CREW: In short, in matters theological, he is the very model of a modern major general.

CAPTAIN: Just look around you. Look at all the boats tied safely to the dock. What's wrong with the dock? It's stable; it's secure.

CREW: I came on board, thinking that we might cross over to the other side.

CAPTAIN: Where would you get an idea like that?

CREW: I'd like to go further, deeper.

CAPTAIN: We've always done it this way. Once a week, we come to the ship, go through the rituals, and memorize procedures from *Roget's Complete Annotated Handbook for Water Safety, Volume Seven*.

CREW: (*to First Mate*) Are you sure he isn't reading from *Sailing for Dummies*?

CAPTAIN: And you know our motto. . . .

FIRST MATE AND CREW: Be prepared?

CAPTAIN: No, no, no. Safety first! But you're getting closer. At least, we're finally getting somewhere.

CREW: That's the problem. We aren't getting anywhere. Let alone to the other side. I came on board to sail—not sit at a dock.

FIRST MATE: I agree. This gets boring, week after week, coming on board, putting on our life preservers, memorizing the handbook, but never untying the dock lines, never really sailing.

CAPTAIN: It depends on your definition of sailing.

CREW: Jibe ho! (*Crew and Captain duck. The First Mate mimes being knocked overboard.*)

CAPTAIN: (*Shouts in panic*) Mayday, mayday. Man, I mean, person overboard!

FIRST MATE: (*"Climbs" back into the boat, with a plastic fish in his mouth*) Aarg! (*Said in a "pirate" voice*) That's it! Weigh the anchor!

CAPTAIN: This is beginning to sound like mutiny.

PIRATES: Aarg! Ahoy, mateys! (*Two persons in business suits and pirate bandannas jump aboard. They speak pirate jargon.*)

CAPTAIN: I am the captain of my fate.

CREW: I didn't know that he was a poet. Besides, it's "captain of my soul."

CAPTAIN: (*To the pirates*) State your identity and your purpose!

FIRST PIRATE: I be the "Scourge of the Seven Seas."

SECOND PIRATE: Aye, ye be! And I be the Jolly Roger, the Blackest Beard, the Scallywag, the Scurvy Dog. . . .

FIRST PIRATE: Enough! Avast ye, landlubber.

SECOND PIRATE: Blimey. Heave ho.

FIRST PIRATE: Blow the man down.

SECOND PIRATE: Marooned!

FIRST PIRATE: Hornswoggled!

CAPTAIN: Hornswoggled? What in heaven's name does that mean?

FIRST PIRATE: (*In normal, not pirate, voice*) This is a hostile offshore, corporate takeover.

CAPTAIN: Shiver me timbers!

FIRST MATE: We're going to sail! Mutiny on the Bounty. Cut the shorelines.

CAPTAIN: You can't. You don't know where the wind will take you. I forbid. . . .

FIRST MATE: Hoist the main sail.

PIRATES: Aye, aye, sir.

FIRST MATE: Unfurl the jib. There's more to sailing than safety first!

CREW: Let's cross to the other side. I feel the wind.

FIRST MATE: Remember our motto. . . .

FIRST PIRATE: Higher. . . .

SECOND PIRATE: Deeper. . . .

CREW: Further!

EVERYONE: We're sailing!

The Checkout Line

COSTUMES/PROPS REQUIRED: Have plastic grocery bags or mime them.

CHARACTERS: Three speaking parts: One person is the "computer" voice; the other two are customers. Add a fourth person to "be" the checkout station if you choose.

SETTING: The automated checkout line at a grocery store. Peter has never used one before; Caroline is behind him in line and offers help.

THEME: Stewardship, learning a new skill. This is a youth fundraising skit written for an announcement before worship.

BACKGROUND: This script is included to Illustrate the various uses of drama. In addition to being a fundraising skit, it could be used at a youth meeting to lead into a discussion on what is an inappropriate item for a Christian to purchase. The other themes of stewardship and of the ability to learn a new skill could also be springboards for lessons and discussion.

DISCUSSION QUESTIONS FOLLOWING THE PERFORMANCE:
❏▶ What made you laugh? Why?
❏▶ With which character did you identify? Why?
❏▶ What line really surprised you? Why?
❏▶ When have you recently had to learn a new skill? What did you learn from this experience?
❏▶ What does this script say about stewardship?
❏▶ What do you picture as the inappropriate item placed in the bag?
❏▶ What spiritual truth or insight did you gain from this play?

DIRECTOR'S NOTES: Peter stands looking confused, trying to figure out how to use the automated checkout. Emma is the automatic bag cart. She stands with her arms out holding empty plastic bags, ready for Peter to fill. Anna, the "computer," stands on the other side of the stage, opposite Peter, at the podium. Anna should begin with a very computer-generated sounding voice and gradually become more human sounding. Anna should never look at Peter and vice versa. Anna should deliver her lines straight to the audience. Peter does not actually have any items to checkout but mimes all of his actions. If you use an "Emma," a person to be the automatic bag cart, she must remain stoic throughout this performance.

The Checkout Line

by Beth Miller

(*Peter stands looking confused, trying to figure out how to use the automated checkout. Emma is the automatic bag cart. She stands with her arms out holding empty plastic bags, ready for Peter to fill. Anna, the "computer," stands on the other side of the stage, opposite Peter, at the podium.*)

ANNA: (*Very computer-generated voice, without emotion*) Hello. Welcome to (*Insert name of the grocery store*). Please push the enter key.

CAROLINE: (*To Peter*) First time?

PETER: Yeah. Boy, this is confusing.

CAROLINE: Want some help?

PETER: Thanks! Don't I know you from somewhere?

ANNA: Please scan your first item.

CAROLINE: I think I've seen you at church. Don't you go to (*your church name*)?

PETER: I sure do.

ANNA: Please place your first item in the bag.

CAROLINE: You need to put it in here.

PETER: Thanks. (*Mimes putting an object into the bag.*)

CAROLINE: I hope you're using the grocery certificates from the church youth program? You know, they raised over nine thousand dollars last year for summer mission trips.

ANNA: Please scan your next item and put it in the bag.

PETER: I can't really afford to give the church any more money.

CAROLINE: Oh, this doesn't cost you anything. It's just a different way of buying your groceries. It's like learning to use these new checkout lanes.

From WORSHIP FEAST: 15 SKETCHES FOR YOUTH GROUP, WORSHIP, & MORE, by Beth Miller. © 2003 by Abingdon Press.

ANNA: Please scan your next item and put it in the bag.

PETER: Haven't you ever heard "There's no such thing as a free ride"? Where does that nine thousand dollars come from then?

ANNA: Please scan your next item and put it in the bag.

CAROLINE: You'd better scan the item! The money comes from the grocery stores. They give five percent of all of the sales back to the youth group.

ANNA: Please remove the unscanned item from your bag.

PETER: What am I supposed to do now?

CAROLINE: Well, on Sunday mornings, you go to the Coffee Hour and find the people selling grocery certificates and write a check to the church youth group. Then they hand you grocery certificates that are as good as cash!

ANNA: Please remove the unscanned item from your bag.

CAROLINE: You can buy them in different dollar amounts, and most of the places give you cash back for the unspent amount. Some give another gift certificate.

ANNA: (*Showing a little emotion*) Please remove the unscanned item from your bag.

PETER: No, I mean about the computer message?

CAROLINE: Oh, right. Take the last item out of your bag and rescan it. (*Peter mimes this.*)

ANNA: Please place the item into the bag.

CAROLINE: It's so easy to use grocery certificates. We helped more than one hundred youth and counselors go on mission trips last summer.

PETER: Next Sunday, I'll buy some and try it. If you can teach me to do this, I can figure out a new way of paying and help the youth program.

ANNA: Please remove the unscanned item from your bag.

PETER: Not this again, what's going on?

CAROLINE: Try scanning it again.

ANNA: That item is not appropriate for (*Enter your denomination/church name*) consumption. Please remove it from your bag!

CAROLINE: See you in church!

From WORSHIP FEAST: 15 SKETCHES FOR YOUTH GROUP, WORSHIP, & MORE, by Beth Miller. © 2003 by Abingdon Press.

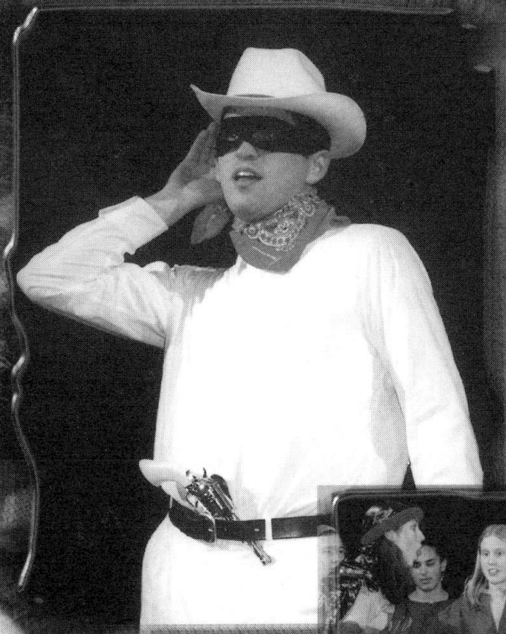

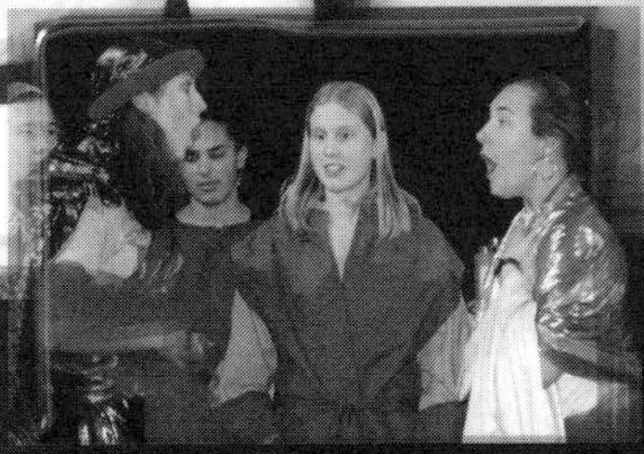

Chapter 4: Scripture Sketches

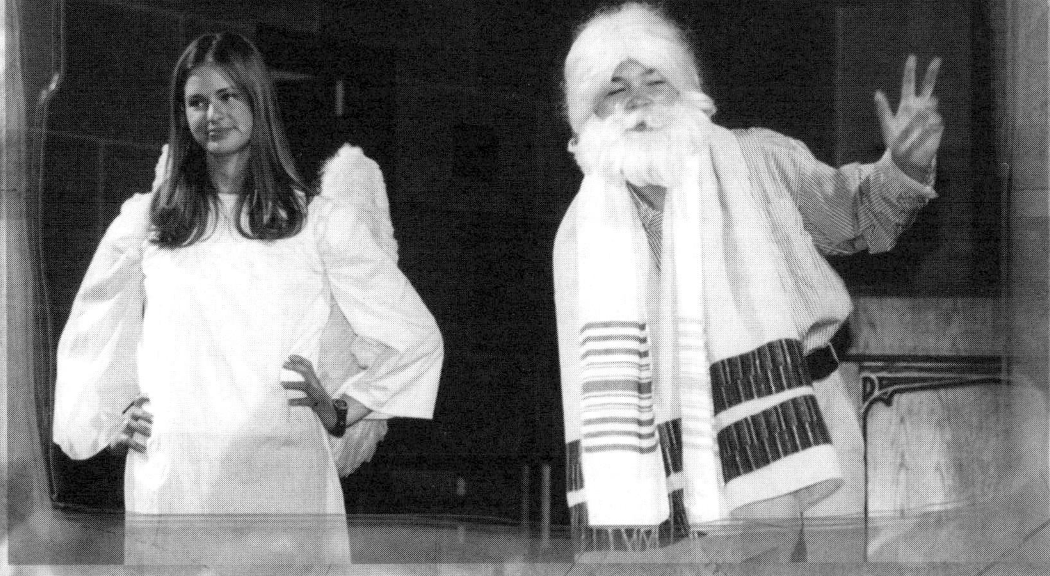

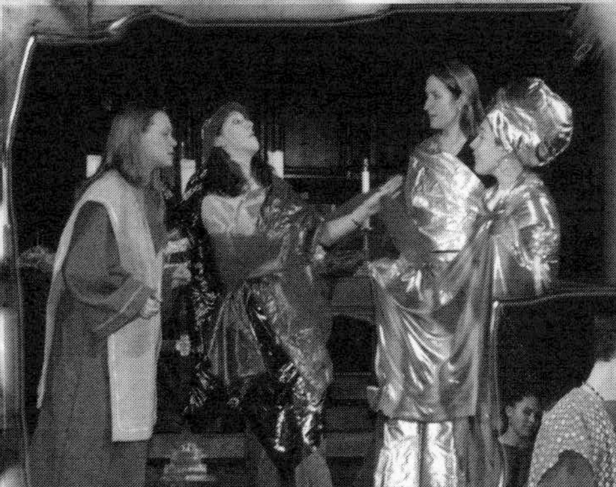

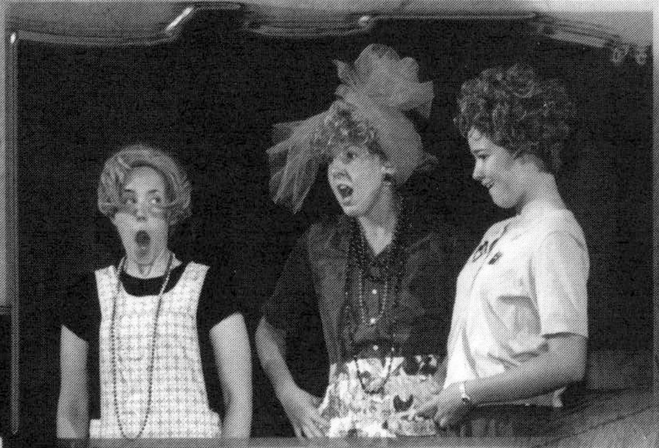

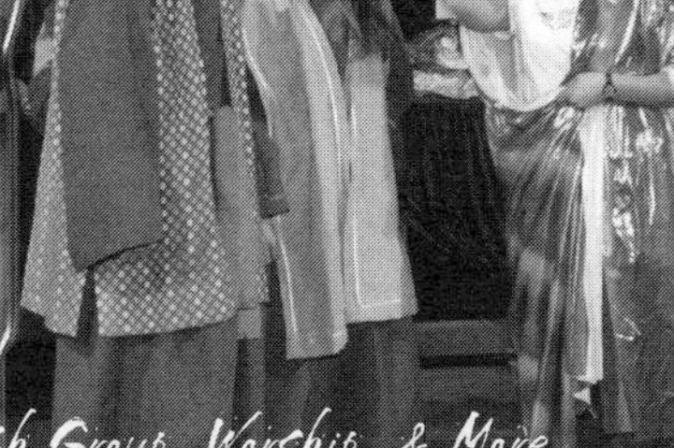

Wendell's Wonderful Weddings

COSTUMES/PROPS REQUIRED: Bridal veil or costume, two "mother of the bride" type dresses or straw hats with flowers, matching cummerbunds and bow ties for Wendell and the servants or a chef's hat for Wendell

CHARACTERS: Six: Three females and three males. Mary, the mother of Jesus; Lydia, the mother of the bride; Sarah, the bride; Wendell, the wedding consultant; and two servants.

SETTING: A hallway outside a wedding reception

SCRIPTURE: Based on John 2:1-11

BACKGROUND: This play was written more than fifteen years ago. On a Saturday night, we had watched *Father of the Bride*. Sunday morning, my husband preached on the text of the wedding at Cana of Galilee. What can I say? The result was this play.

Often we forget that the people in the biblical stories were human. They had the same feelings as we do. The Bible story on which this sketch is based was the first of Jesus' miracles. It certainly must have come as quite a surprise to those involved, especially to his mother. Mary doesn't seem too pleased with Jesus' response. Mary was a Jewish mother. We had fun with that in this script. Take care not to play Wendell as effeminate. Fussy, particular, and demanding are the words to describe his character.

You may want to read the Scripture reference to the audience just before the performance. The King James translation is the only major translation to use the word *firkin* instead of gallons.

DISCUSSION QUESTIONS FOLLOWING THE PERFORMANCE:
☐▶ What made you laugh? Why?
☐▶ With which character did you identify? Why?
☐▶ What surprised you about the portrayal of this story?
☐▶ Have you ever thought about the amount of water (162 gallons) turned into wine?
☐▶ What does wine symbolize in this story?
☐▶ What did Mary expect of Jesus?
☐▶ What new insight did you gain from this play?

DIRECTOR'S NOTES: Timing of entrances and exits are important in this sketch to keep the tempo building. The bride's opening lines have to be extremely exaggerated. The servant roles are meant to be opposites, using the Shakespearean technique of having a smart servant and a simple servant.

Wendell's Wonderful Weddings

by Dale Dobson, Beth Miller and David Schwaninger

MARY: Lydia, the wedding was lovely! Sarah was such a beautiful bride.

LYDIA: Oh, Mary, I never thought I'd see the day . . . my little Sarah, standing under the wedding canopy with Joshua. Where have the years gone?

MARY: I always hoped that Jesus would find a nice Jewish girl and settle down someday.

LYDIA: What can I say? Jesus has always been somewhat of a radical. I'm sure you wish he would stay at home more. He always seems to be traipsing around the countryside.

MARY: I really do. That's why it meant so much to me that you would invite him to Sarah's wedding. I'm rather embarrassed that he brought along his friends.

LYDIA: Oh, think nothing of it. Jesus is like part of the family. His friends are our friends. (*This is said with sweetness, followed by . . .*) Who are those fellows, anyway? I don't recognize any of them as local boys?

MARY: Some are from Galilee, Capernaum and beyond the Jordan—(*name of the town you where are performing*), I think.

(*Sarah runs down the center aisle, distraught.*)

SARAH: Mother! (*Exaggerate the word "wine."*) We've run out of WINE!

LYDIA: (*Exaggerate the word "whine."*) It doesn't sound like you've run out of WHINE, Sarah.

SARAH: Really, Mother. I'm a married woman now!

LYDIA: Sarah, please calm down. I'll check with Wendell, the wedding consultant. I'm sure everything is under control.

SARAH: Dear "Auntie Mary," please DO something! She never takes me seriously.

From WORSHIP FEAST: 15 SKETCHES FOR YOUTH GROUP, WORSHIP, & MORE, by Beth Miller. © 2003 by Abingdon Press.

MARY: Now, Sarah, I'm sure everything will be fine. Try to relax a little and enjoy everything.

SARAH: We've been planing this wedding for over a year, it's THE event of the season. (*She starts to exit.*) How embarrassing—to run out of wine! Oh no, I broke a nail! My wedding is ruined! (*Sees Wendell coming down the aisle toward them.*) You, you're the wedding receptionist! DO SOMETHING! (*Exits.*)

WENDELL: (*To Sarah*) I AM NOT a receptionist! This is a wedding reception. (*Realizes that Sarah is gone; addresses Mary and Lydia.*) I, Wendell, am the wedding consultant. If you are having a wedding, consult me. When people adhere to Wendell's consultation, problems do not arise.

LYDIA: Wendell, Sarah says the supply of wine is running out.

WENDELL: This put us right over the limit. I recommended that you increase the wine order. We had barely enough. But would you listen to Wendell? Nooo. Then you invite this Jesus fellow at the last minute . . . and he brings along all his scruffy little friends.

MARY: If you'll excuse me for a minute, Lydia, I need to find Jesus and speak to him.

LYDIA: Mary, please don't think this has anything to do with Jesus. (*Wendell raises his eyebrows and "huffs" at this.*)

MARY: I'll be right back. (*Mary exits one side, while two servants enter from the opposite side.*)

SERVANT 1: The guests are grumbling, Ma'am.

SERVANT 2: It seems the supply of wine is running quite low and . . . well. . . .

SERVANT 1: The party's just begun.

WENDELL: My plans have never been so completely derailed.

LYDIA: What can I say? Just tell the band to play a little louder; and please push the miniature kosher hot dogs. We have plenty of those.

WENDELL: I'm sorry about the little ham rolls. I don't know what I was thinking?

SERVANT 1: Push the band members, eat the ham rolls, and could you hot dogs play louder?

From WORSHIP FEAST: 15 SKETCHES FOR YOUTH GROUP, WORSHIP, & MORE, by Beth Miller. © 2003 by Abingdon Press.

SERVANT 2: Whatever you say. Don't worry, Ma'am. I'll remember everything. (*Both servants exit.*)

WENDELL: My reputation as "Wendell's Wonderful Weddings" could be irrevocably tarnished. I'll never do a wedding in Cana again. (*Wendell exits one direction, as Mary enters the other.*)

LYDIA: Well, Mary, what did Jesus say?

MARY: I can't believe it. . . . He said, "Woman, my time has not yet come."

LYDIA: What can I say? It must be those fellows he's been hanging around with . . . (*Mary interrupts.*)

MARY: Can you imagine? To me, his mother, he said: "Woman, my time has not yet come." "Oh, Mom, is the pizza here yet?" Sorry, son, you see the delivery person's time has not yet come. "Mom, it's laundry day; and I'm all out of clean socks!" Oh no! Sorry, son. You see MY time has not yet come. To me, who raised him, he said, " WOMAN, MY TIME HAS NOT YET COME! Sorry, Jesus, I wouldn't want you to do anything before your "time." (*Servants enter toward the end of her speech.*)

SERVANT 1: Sorry to interrupt, Ma'am, but Jesus . . .

MARY: Jesus! What did he do now?

SERVANT 2: Ma'am, Jesus told us to collect all the water from the finger bowls and pour them into these six huge stone water jars.

SERVANT 1: But we thought we should check with you first.

MARY: Mind you, do whatever he tells you.

SERVANT 1: He told us to fill the six jars to the rim with the water.

SERVANT 2: Are you aware of how much water this would be? Each jar holds three firkins. There are nine gallons in a firkin. That would be twenty-seven gallons of water per jar, times six jars. . . . That makes one hundred sixty-two gallons!

SERVANT 1: WHOA! That's a lot of water to haul around! (*To Servant 2*) Go ahead, tell her the best part. Go ahead.

SERVANT 2: Jesus said that after we had filled the jars with water, to draw some out and take it to Wendell.

SERVANT 1: What a kidder!

From WORSHIP FEAST: 15 SKETCHES FOR YOUTH GROUP, WORSHIP, & MORE, by Beth Miller. © 2003 by Abingdon Press.

LYDIA: What can I say? Just do whatever he tells you.

SERVANT 1: Well, OK. We'd better start hauling those firkin jars. (*They exit.*)

MARY: Lydia, you surprise me. Why did you tell them to do what Jesus said?

LYDIA: What can I say? I trust him. Let's get back to the celebration.

(*Sarah runs down the center aisle. Mary and Lydia turn away to go the opposite direction, but Sarah stops them.*)

SARAH: Mother, it's absolutely wonderful! The band is wonderful, the food is wonderful, and the wine—the wine is wonderful! The whole town is raving about the wine. (*She starts to exit, and meets Wendell.*) Wendell, oh, Wendell, it's wonderful! Thank you! It's wonderful! (*They hug and dance as she exits.*)

WENDELL: (*To Sarah*) But, of course! (*To the women*) Wherever did you get this wine? This wine is divine! (*Lydia and Mary whisper something about finger bowls.*) I'll just have to eat a little humble pie and apologize. Everyone Wendell knows puts their good wine out first; and then when everyone has had plenty to drink, brings out the poor stuff. But you, you have saved the best for the last.

MARY AND LYDIA: What can we say?

From WORSHIP FEAST: 15 SKETCHES FOR YOUTH GROUP, WORSHIP, & MORE, by Beth Miller. © 2003 by Abingdon Press.

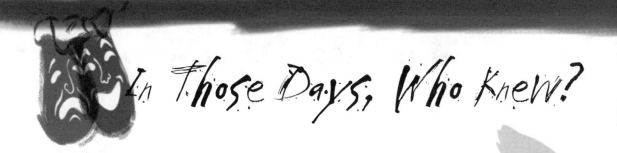

In Those Days, Who Knew?

COSTUMES/PROPS REQUIRED:
- Zechariah: Prayer shawl, yarmulke, gray wig and beard (a Santa wig and beard works), a large sign with the name *John* handprinted on it
- Gabriel: Angel costume with feather wings (available from Oriental Trading Company)
- Elizabeth: Old sweater, gray wig, apron
- Ruth and Esther: Gaudy dresses, aprons, loud jewelry, gray wigs, scarves

CHARACTERS: Five: Four females and one male. Elizabeth and Zechariah; the angel Gabriel (a female, who can double as one of Elizabeth's friends); Ruth and Esther, two of Elizabeth's' bothersome neighbors

SETTING: The first and third scenes are in the home of Zechariah and Elizabeth. The second scene is before the altar of incense at the Temple.

SCRIPTURE: Based on Luke 1:5-25

BACKGROUND: This play is another in the original Strangely Warmed Players' repertoire. Every time I heard this Scripture read, I wondered what took place between Zechariah and Gabriel. Zechariah tests Gabriel's patience, and the result is Zechariah's inability to talk until John is born. Dale, David, and I did some improvisation one night and came up with this sketch.

Miracles were abundant at the time of Jesus' birth. Perhaps they still are, but we are just as unaware as the original characters were in this story. They probably did not understand the significance of what was happening in their lives. In those days, who knew?

You may want to read the Scripture reference to the audience just before the performance.

DISCUSSION QUESTIONS FOLLOWING THE PERFORMANCE:
❏▶ What made you laugh? Why?
❏▶ With which character did you identify? Why?
❏▶ What surprised you about the portrayal of this story?
❏▶ What expectations did Elizabeth's neighbors have for her baby?
❏▶ What expectations do we have of others?
❏▶ What new insight did you gain from this play?

DIRECTOR'S NOTES: Elizabeth is the narrator. In the opening and final scenes, she speaks directly to the audience. She does not need to leave the stage entirely for the Zechariah and Gabriel scene but can move to one side and sit on the edge of the stage. She mimes preparing supper, with her back to Zechariah. Gabriel should begin very playfully, taking time to build her feelings of frustration with Zechariah. When Zechariah needs to take time, he mimes writing the name *John* on a sign. Then he holds up the sign for the audience to read, pauses, then exits. Ruth and Esther's lines must be delivered almost on top of one another.

In Those Days, Who Knew?

by Dale Dobson, Beth Miller and David Schwaninger

ELIZABETH: Hello. I'm here to tell you a story. It happened a long time ago to me and my husband, Zechariah. Now don't go looking in the Old Testament. That's a completely different Zechariah altogether. Our story was told by a nice young fellow named Luke. It all started when my husband was tending incense in the Temple. Such an honor—tending incense. And to think, it all started right here under our noses. But in those days, who knew?

(*Elizabeth exits or stands to the side of the stage. Zechariah enters first, followed by the angel Gabriel.*)

GABRIEL: Psssst.

ZECHARIAH: Hmmm? Who's there? I can hardly see a thing with all this smoke. At my age, I can hardly see the smoke.

GABRIEL: Zechariah, I have come to bring you good news.

ZECHARIAH: Terrific, I could use some news that is good these days. What is it?

GABRIEL: Guess!

ZECHARIAH: Let's see . . . it's three o'clock. You've come to release me early from incense duty?

GABRIEL: No, try again.

ZECHARIAH: Ah, you've come to help me scrub down the sacrificial altar then, eh?

GABRIEL: No. One more guess.

ZECHARIAH: I don't know. My wife, she's going to have a baby, I suppose?

GABRIEL: Bingo!

ZECHARIAH: No. For that, you've got the wrong place. Try Saint Michael's down the street.

GABRIEL: No, I mean, you are right about your wife and the baby.

ZECHARIAH: Sure, we'll be the oldest parents in Judea. (*Pretending to address a third person, who isn't there*) "Honey, get me my walker. I'm going to play catch with Junior."

From WORSHIP FEAST: 15 SKETCHES FOR YOUTH GROUP, WORSHIP, & MORE, by Beth Miller. © 2003 by Abingdon Press.

GABRIEL: Exactly.

ZECHARIAH: You're serious, aren't you?

GABRIEL: Of course, dead serious.

ZECHARIAH: Good news is one thing; a good joke is another. This is a joke, eh? A rather poor one, I think. I am old. Elizabeth is old. We couldn't raise a kid with a forklift.

GABRIEL: Youth drifts on the waves of passion, while age soars on the wings of wisdom.

ZECHARIAH: Where are you from, Kid—Hallmark?

GABRIEL: Look, Zech, your prayers have been answered. You're going to be a papa.

ZECHARIAH: A pooped papa. I'm too pooped to be a papa. Kid, I don't know who put you up to this; but it is just pain dumb!

GABRIEL: Dumb?

ZECHARIAH: Dumb!

GABRIEL: All right, fine. Have it your way—dumb!

(*Zechariah is stricken dumb by a snap of Gabriel's fingers. Zechariah tries to speak but can't.*)

GABRIEL: Well, now that I can get a word in edgewise, allow me to introduce myself. I am Gabriel, one of the Lord's representatives in this territory. I was sent to offer you a child, a son. You are to name him John. That's J-O-H-N. When all this has come to pass, your voice will return. (*Gabriel begins to exit, stops, and addresses the audience.*) This has been a public service announcement!

(*Elizabeth assumes a position on stage, looking away from Zechariah. She mimes stirring a pot over a stove.*)

ELIZABETH: So you're finally home, smelling all of incense as usual. Late, but finally home. Take off your shawl, and I'll have dinner ready in a minute. (*She waits for a response. Hearing none, she continues.*) You're awfully quiet today, dear. Any news from the Temple?

ZECHARIAH: (*Nods and tries to relate with his arms the enormity of what happened.*)

ELIZABETH: We're too old for charades, dear. You've got a tongue in your head, so use it.

ZECHARIAH: (*Points to the sky and flaps his arms, trying to indicate the angels' appearance.*)

ELIZABETH: Some birds flew into the Temple? Did anyone sacrifice them?

FROM WORSHIP FEAST: 15 SKETCHES FOR YOUTH GROUP, WORSHIP, & MORE, by Beth Miller. © 2003 by Abingdon Press.

ZECHARIAH: (*Shakes his head no and tries again. Points to himself, then points to Elizabeth, and indicates a pregnant form.*)

ELIZABETH: Neither of us is getting fat on your salary, dear!

ZECHARIAH: (*Cradles an imaginary baby in his arms, and then hugs Elizabeth.*)

ELIZABETH: Oh, baby, I love you too!

ZECHARIAH: (*He shrugs, gives up, and exits. Elizabeth addresses the audience.*)

ELIZABETH: My husband had been serving me breakfast in bed. A good man, he is, but a cook he should never be! I thought that it was just indigestion. About four months later, I figured it out for myself. I was in a family way. Better late than never, thank the Lord. My young cousin Mary was also with child. She came to visit me for a few months. I tell you, nothing crosses the generation gap like a miracle. But in those days, who knew? (*Two older Jewish friends enter as Elizabeth delivers these lines.*) You'll have to excuse me for a minute. It seems the entire village is rather amused with my situation. And my friends insist on having a baby shower.

RUTH: So what are you going to name the baby, Elizabeth?

ESTHER: Zechariah, of course, after his father.

ELIZABETH: No, his name is to be John!

RUTH AND ESTHER: John?

ESTHER: But you don't have any relatives named John!

RUTH: I've never heard of such a thing. Who names a baby John? Sounds like a tax-collector or some other kind of riff-raff.

ESTHER: Why don't you pick a more traditional name, like Malachi . . . or Hezekiah?

RUTH: Haggai!

ESTHER: Haggai is a very popular name this year.

RUTH: John? There aren't nearly enough syllables. No music to it at all.

ESTHER: Elizabeth, get Zechariah in here. He'll settle everything.

ELIZABETH: Zechy dear, can you come in here a minute?

(*Zechariah enters, carrying a large "tablet" and a marker.*)

RUTH: Zechariah, you must speak to your wife. (*He shrugs.*) Tell her what the child should be named?

(*He mimes writing in large letters J-O-H-N. Then he holds up the sign for the audience to read.*)

From Worship Feast: 15 Sketches for Youth Group, Worship, & More, by Beth Miller. © 2003 by Abingdon Press.

ELIZABETH: It's a sign! (*Zechariah exits.*)

RUTH: All right, fine. But what kind of child is this going to be?

ELIZABETH: Maybe he'll be a doctor.

ESTHER: A doctor? Dr. John?

RUTH: Sounds like a musician.

ESTHER: A politician—maybe he's going to be a politician.

(*Ruth's lines are said to Esther as the two women exit.*)

RUTH: A no good bum, living in the desert, dressed in wild animal skins eating honey and locust. Mark my words.

ELIZABETH: And so, with the help of my gabby friends, the news spread through all the hills of Judea. The baby shower was a great success. Esther gave me a beautiful blanket; and Ruth, the old yenta, gave me a year's supply of Geritol. My husband finally started to talk again. Funny, it happened almost the very moment our son, John, was born. John became a Baptist. Trust me, I couldn't have been happier if he had become a lawyer. (*Pause.*) Mary's son? Well, you know that story. And to think, it all happened right under our noses. But in those days, who knew?

Wake Up, Adam!

COSTUMES/PROPS REQUIRED: A large plate with an imaginary cake on it, a bench, pillows, a quilt for Adam to hide under, a clock, crumpled clothes, athletic socks, a tennis shoe, a telephone

CHARACTERS: Requires a cast of three: one male and two females. Adam's Mother, Adam, and Eve

SETTING: The scene takes place in Adam's bedroom—a menagerie of animal cages in desperate need of cleaning. On one side is an imaginary window, through which Eve arrives. On the other side is the door.

THEME: Based on Genesis 2:15-20; 3:6-10

BACKGROUND: A hilarious take-off on the Adam and Eve temptation story. Adam's mother takes on the role of God. Adam's mother is urging him to organize, label everything, and clean up the animal cages.

You may want to read the Scripture reference to the audience just before the performance.

DISCUSSION QUESTIONS FOLLOWING THE PERFORMANCE:
☐▶ With which character did you identify? Why?
☐▶ What surprised you about the portrayal of this story?
☐▶ What did the cake symbolize?
☐▶ In what ways was Adam's mother similar to God? How was she different?
☐▶ What were the consequences for Eve after eating the cake?
☐▶ What new insight did you gain from this play?

DIRECTOR'S NOTES: Block Adam's mother to one side of the stage. She could be at a microphone. All of the action should be mimed. The actors playing Adam and Eve need to block the location of each animal on stage so that their miming will be believable.

Wake Up, Adam!

by Megan Jo Crumm

(Lights out on stage. Adam is asleep on a bench, a quilt draped over him, a couple of pillows under his head. Some kind of bedside clock is nearby. Beneath Adam and his quilt are hidden some crumpled clothes, including some athletic socks, a tennis shoe, and a telephone.)

(A light turns on.)

MOM: (*Off stage*) Aaaaaaa-daaaaam! (*No reaction from Adam other than a slight movement*) Aaaaaaa-daaaaam! Wake up!

ADAM: Huh?

MOM: Adam! It's Monday!

ADAM: (*Waving his hand in a disgusted gesture*) Ugh!

MOM: A new week's beginning! Come on!

ADAM: Awwwww!

MOM: Don't make me yell, Adam! It's Monday! You know what I always say: A whole new world's waiting for you!

ADAM: Mooommm! Come on. Just give me five more minutes! Turn off the lights, Mom! Come on! The light?

MOM: Adam, the light's good for you! You don't want to live like a mole! Let's goooo!

ADAM: (*Adam throws off one of his pillows. Then, slowly sits up, looking tired. He reaches out and takes a good look at his bedside clock.*) Mooommm! I don't have to get up for another hour!

MOM: You've got a lot of work to do today, young man!

ADAM: (*Adam makes a sour face and mouths silently to the audience: "Young man?"*)

MOM: To start with, you have to clean your room. It's a mess since those animals moved in!

ADAM: I can handle it, Mom.

MOM: It's an out-of-control zoo up there!

ADAM: No it isn't. It's just the fish tank, the ferret, the tarantula, a couple of toads, an iguana, and . . .

MOM: The Python!

ADAM: (*Grinning*) Yeah, the snake!

MOM: And those rats!

ADAM: Yeah, and the rats.

MOM: Fourteen rats and counting!

ADAM: So, they had babies, Ma! I thought they were both male!

MOM: Adam, are you trying to tell me that you don't know about nature? We told you all about the birds and the bees!

ADAM: (*Adam makes another sour face and mouths to the audience: "The birds and the bees?"*)

MOM: What was that, young man?

ADAM: Nothing!

MOM: Because I've got a whole stack of those plastic bins and tubs. I want you to get everything organized up there! (*Adam shakes his head.*) And I want everything labeled! We've been talking about this for a long time. I want everything named and numbered so that you can find things in that—that—pigsty of yours.

ADAM: Mom, I know where everything is!

MOM: It's chaos up there!

ADAM: It's paradise, Mom! My own little paradise!

MOM: No more arguments, Adam! Get the tubs. Pick up the junk. Sort it out! We need some order!

From WORSHIP FEAST: 15 SKETCHES FOR YOUTH GROUP, WORSHIP, & MORE, by Beth Miller. © 2003 by Abingdon Press.

(Adam stands up and picks up his quilt, revealing a pile of crumpled clothes. He picks up a smelly sock, nearly faints, and then finds an old tennis shoe. His expression tells us that the shoe, too, really smells. He throws it off stage. Someone off stage makes a thump.)

MOM: What's that noise?

ADAM: That's the sound of order, Mom! *(He continues sorting.)*

MOM: Make sure you feed all those animals!

ADAM: But, Mooommm!

MOM: Remember, back when I agreed to give you some of your pets in the first place? *(Imitating Adam)* And I'll take care of them, and play with them, and feed them. . . .

ADAM: Yeah, but I'm the one who's hungry!

MOM: OK. . . . Well, you know you can eat anything you want in the fridge. *(Pause.)* Just don't touch that Black Forest Chocolate Cheesecake on the kitchen counter!

ADAM: *(Suddenly looking interested)* Black Forest Chocolate Cheesecake? That one you made with the dark chocolate layers and the frosting on top with the black cherries? THAT Black Forest Chocolate Cheesecake? *(Adam sounds hungry.)*

MOM: Yes! You can have whatever else you want in the kitchen. Just don't touch that cake!

ADAM: Why not?

MOM: Just because!

ADAM: Mommmmmm, that's not a reason!

MOM: Because I made it for something special. And because I SAID SO! Just don't touch it!

ADAM: *(Throwing up his hands)* OK! OK! I'll . . . *(Thinking, then hitting on a great idea)* . . . I'll eat some of that cold pizza!

MOM: Ugh! Adam, you know how I hate that idea.

ADAM: And a Coke!

MOM: For breakfast?

ADAM: Yeah, and some Barbecue Doritos!

MOM: Oh, Adam, that's disgusting! All the good food I provide for you in this house, and you eat that trash!

ADAM: Well, I could eat. . . .

MOM: Never mind! All I'm asking is that you don't stick your fingers in that cake.

ADAM: (*Shrugs.*) OK! (*Keeps sorting through the crumpled clothes until he finds a phone and stops to dial a number.*)

MOM: What are you doing now?

ADAM: I'm bored! I'm calling a friend!

MOM: Who?

ADAM: A girl.

MOM: What? Who?

ADAM: She's just a girl! I was just thinking . . . maybe . . .

MOM: Adam, we've talked about this! You're not old enough to date! I'll let you know when I think you're old enough!

ADAM: (*Crosses his arms wearily*) Mooommm! I'm talking about hanging out. Mom, I can't be alone forever! (*Moves to one side and mimes opening a window.*)

MOM: What's going on up there?

ADAM: Opening my window! Letting some air in up here. OK? (*Through the window comes a girl. She's wearing a sweatshirt labeled in big block letters: EVE. They stealthily move into the room. Adam motions to her to keep quiet.*)

ADAM: (*Whispers*) Let me close the door! (*Sound of door closing as he moves to close it. Hastily picks up a crumpled pair of socks and tosses them to one side.*) Just cleaning up the old room and I got bored, y' know? Glad you could come over.

EVE: (*Looking around*) Wow! Your room is awesome! You've got some cool animals. I don't care what your Mom says. Your room is great!

FROM WORSHIP FEAST: 15 SKETCHES FOR YOUTH GROUP, WORSHIP, & MORE, by Beth Miller. © 2003 by Abingdon Press.

ADAM: (*Rushing around and pointing things out.*) This one is Emerald, the iguana. These are John, Paul, George, and Ringo. They're beetles. This one . . . well, I don't have a name for him yet.

EVE: How about Fido? He could be a . . . cat! No, a dog. He could be a dog!

ADAM: Fido the dog?

EVE: That sounds great! He even looks like a dog! (*Looking at the python*) And what's your name?

ADAM: I was thinking about calling him Monty. Monty the Python (*Eve is clearly not paying attention; she's talking to the snake.*) Eve? Are you listening? Hey, Eve? (*Taps her on the shoulder.*)

EVE: (*Sweetly*) You know, I'm getting a little hungry. I looked through your patio door on the way in, and there's a killer cake on your table.

ADAM: Not supposed to touch it.

EVE: (*Smiles*) Oh. Well, it looks sooo good . And you know how much I like chocolate.

ADAM: I told my Mom, you know . . .

EVE: Adam, I really love chocolate. (*Adam sighs deeply, looks at the audience and shrugs. He exits.*)

EVE: (*Looking where the snake is*) Monty Python. What a funny name! You know, reptiles aren't all that bad!

ADAM: (*Proudly displaying the fruits of his theft—the [imaginary] cake*) How's this?

EVE: (*Miming taking a big forkful*) Mmmm. Try it! Adam, there's nothing better than chocolate cheesecake for breakfast! (*He mimes taking a bite.*) Except maybe cold pizza and Coke. (*Adam nods and smiles. They eat.*)

EVE: (*Her smile fades*) Adam, it really stinks in here.

ADAM: I hadn't really thought about it. I guess it does.

EVE: I didn't notice it when I walked in; but everything is really dusty, and the water in all the fish tanks is green.

ADAM: Well, I haven't cleaned the bird cages in a while, and I really should clean out the salamander tank.

From Worship Feast: 15 Sketches for Youth Group, Worship, & More, by Beth Miller. © 2003 by Abingdon Press.

EVE: (*Not paying attention to him*) You need to do something about that snake, too. He smells AWFUL.

ADAM: (*Sort of hurt*) I thought you liked the python.

EVE: I've changed my mind. He stinks.

ADAM: But . . . I spend a lot of time in this room. I like this room! I . . .

EVE: (*Interrupting*) Adam, there's got to be more than this, you know? A bigger world than snakes and pizza and e-mail?

ADAM: Maybe.

EVE: At least one that smells better.

MOM: (*Off stage, loud, upset, and sad*) Aaaaa-daaaaam, my caaaaake!

ADAM: (*Pauses, looks at the cake plate. Looks at Eve. Eve eyes him. She doesn't like what's happening. She's disgusted.*) Mooommm, I'll talk to you in a minute!

MOM: Adam, that was for a special dinner! I don't even have time to make another one. Adam, you really disappoint me!

ADAM: (*To Eve*) You'd better go, I guess.

EVE: Adam, you've got a lot to sort out—and we're not talking socks. By the way, that chocolate is to DIE FOR! (*Eve slips back out the window. Adam looks around at his room.*)

MOM: Adam! Are you coming to talk to me about this—this mess with the cake? I thought you were more responsible than this. (*Adam sinks down and crawls back under his covers.*) Adam! Don't think you can hide from me! (*Finally, Adam pulls the covers completely over his head.*) Adam? (*Slower and concerned*) Adam?

From WORSHIP FEAST: 15 SKETCHES FOR YOUTH GROUP, WORSHIP, & MORE, by Beth Miller. © 2003 by Abingdon Press.

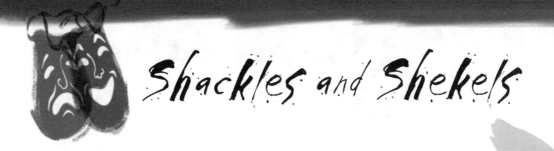

Shackles and Shekels

COSTUMES/PROPS REQUIRED: Two plastic pig noses, chains, hats for the human characters, bib overalls for Pig Herder, a ripped hospital gown for Legion

CHARACTERS: Requires a cast of seven: All roles can be cast as either male or female; however, Legion is written as a female. Cast includes: Squeakers and Jeepers (the pigs), Pig Herder, Boss (the owner of the pigs), Tourist Official, Shackle Maker, and Legion.

SETTING: The scene takes place on the edge of the cliff in the hillside country of the Gerasenes, overlooking the lake. Jesus has just cast demons into a herd of pigs; and all but two of the pigs have run over a cliff, into the sea, and were drowned. Squeakers and Jeepers, the two remaining pigs, begin the play by describing what has just happened.

SCRIPTURE: Based on Mark 5:1-17

BACKGROUND: This play is another in the original Strangely Warmed Players' repertoire. This is not one of those favorite Bible passages that shouts, "Act this out on stage!" Most of us are uncomfortable with stories about demons and pigs leaping over cliffs. However, it is one of the few stories where, following a miracle performed by Jesus, the town's people beg him to leave their city.

How often are we uncomfortable with change? Even in the church, do we allow people to be transformed, to be healed and made whole? Or are we more comfortable with the status quo? The title for this play comes from our theory that, perhaps, one of the reasons Jesus is asked to leave is that he upset the local economy and culture. The locals were comfortable with Legion in shackles, as long as they were making their shekels.

You may want to read the Scripture reference to the audience just before the performance.

DISCUSSION QUESTIONS FOLLOWING THE PERFORMANCE:
❏▶ With which character did you identify? Why?
❏▶ What surprised you about the portrayal of this story?
❏▶ What might the shackles symbolize?
❏▶ Why were the locals upset about Legion's healing?
❏▶ In what ways do we suppress change in people?
❏▶ What are the demons that oppress the world today?
❏▶ What new insight did you gain from this play?

DIRECTOR'S NOTES: When Legion enters, block the scene so that she is behind the Boss and that the rest of the cast is on the other side of the stage. Everyone sees Legion, except the Boss. The Boss is so consumed with anger over losing his pig herd that he can't hear her. Have fun with all the swine references. Building the final scene is imperative.

Shackles and Shekels

by Dale Dobson, Beth Miller, and David Schwaninger

JEEPERS: Jeepers! I can't believe what I just saw!

SQUEAKERS: It was horrible. One minute I was talking to Madge about how she and Herb and the piglets were doing; and the next thing I know, her eyes are twirling around like pinwheels and she's leaping off this cliff and into the sea of Galilee.

JEEPERS: Jeepers! The whole herd! Blanche, Janelle, Muffy. . . . One step too many, and now they're all gone!

SQUEAKERS: Now Gidget always was a little dingy, but when she started doin' the Mamba toward the edge of the cliff. . . .

JEEPERS: Jeepers! I can't believe it! I just can't believe it!

SQUEAKERS: Two thousand of them . . . that's a lot of pork to go over the edge.

JEEPERS AND SQUEAKERS: Jeepers!

(*Herder and Boss enter.*)

HERDER: It's like I've been trying to tell yah, boss. . . . One minute—calm as any herd of pigs I've ever seen; then the next thing, they're completely amuck, running berserk over the cliff and into the sea of Galilee.

BOSS: Yea, I see.

HERDER: Well, at least two of them decided not to take the pork belly plunge. . . . Yea, I guess you're right—they're not much are they?

BOSS: Couldn't you have stopped them?

HERDER: I guess I could have thrown my body in front of 'em.

BOSS: Well, if you couldn't stop the herd, do you, at least, have any idea what caused it? (*Herder looks perplexed and shrugs his shoulders.*) Oh, come on now! Don't you have any idea?

HERDER: I don't know. . . . Well . . . maybe. . . . Maybe they just got tired of living with the thought of a hole in the ozone, or they were worried about the economy. This cloning thing really has the herd upset, and (*insert some current event*). And I don't know about you, but I still can't program my VCR.

BOSS: There's no logical reason for an entire herd of pigs to go crackers at once. . . . We're not talking lemmings here, ya know!

HERDER: I know, Boss; but there was this stranger talking to Legion.

BOSS: What do you mean talking to Legion? Are you crazier than he is? Why, no one has talked with that fruitcake in years!

SQUEAKERS: I think the that Herder is right. There was someone talking with the Looney One.

BOSS: No one has gone near the guy. And if they do, he attacks them. He has been known to do that on several occasions. No one talks to Legion!

HERDER: I know all that, Boss. But this guy was from out of town, across the Jordan. (*Shackle Maker and Tourist Official come on stage, quite excited, and interrupt the Herder.*)

SHACKLE MAKER: What's this we hear about hogs gone wild?

TOURIST OFFICIAL: Pigs going crazy?

HERDER: You've heard?

JEEPERS: We're not the herd! Two pigs don't make a herd!

SHACKLE MAKER: The news is all over town.

TOURIST OFFICIAL: Is it true?

HERDER: If you'll step over here, you can take a look for yourself. But I'm warnin' ya—it ain't a pretty sight.

BOSS: According to my pig herder, all of them just committed sooey-cide!

JEEPERS: What does he mean ALL OF THEM? We're part of the herd!

SQUEAKERS: (*To Herder*) That's right! Go ahead and ignore us!

HERDER: And then their eyes started looking funny and. . . . (*Boss interrupts.*)

BOSS: And he seems to think that it all has something to do with some stranger talking to Legion.

From WORSHIP FEAST: 15 SKETCHES FOR YOUTH GROUP, WORSHIP, & MORE, by Beth Miller. © 2003 by Abingdon Press.

SHACKLE MAKER: Legion? You haven't seen him lately, have you?

HERDER: Well, as a matter of fact, I just. . . . (*Boss interrupts.*)

BOSS: No, haven't seen him. Why do you ask?

SHACKLE MAKER: No urgent reason. But I do have these new shackles to try out on him. He broke the last pair I made.

TOURIST OFFICIAL: By the way, Charlie, how many pairs does that make now?

SHACKLE MAKER: I lost track months ago. All I know is, the village council keeps wanting shackles; so I keep making them.

TOURIST OFFICIAL: And you just keep raking in the shekels for the shackles; don't you, Charlie? You ought to start making them ahead of time.

SHACKLE MAKER: I have. I have. I've got twelve pair all set to go—oven-fired and ankle hungry.

HERDER: Hey, Boss, excuse me for thinkin' out loud. But what about the pigs?

BOSS: What about the pigs? You're the only witness, witless!

HERDER: It's like I've been tryin' to tell you—this guy, kind of quiet, talkin' to Legion.

BOSS: Hogwash!

SHACKLE MAKER: Mother of Mercy, I've been measuring that maniac for manacles for more months than my memory maintains!

EVERYONE: That's amazing!

SHACKLE MAKER: That's the script! And he's never said more than two words to me. . . . And those were both rude!

TOURIST OFFICIAL: You expect us to believe that Legion was having a normal conversation with a stranger?

SHACKLE MAKER: What a load of slop!

TOURIST OFFICIAL: We might as well believe in aliens!

SHACKLE MAKER: Or the tooth fairy!

HERDER: Hey, what about the tooth fairy?

BOSS: All I know is that I lost a lot of money when I lost those pigs.

SHACKLE MAKER: Maybe it was something they ate. . . .

TOURIST OFFICIAL: Or drank?

HERDER: I'm tellin' ya—this stranger was talkin' to Legion, and suddenly the pigs run berserk over the cliff.

BOSS: There's no connection, no connection at all. (*During this speech, Legion comes on stage and begins tapping Boss on the shoulder. The others see Legion and back away, while Boss remains oblivious.*) I just can't see how some guy from out of town, talking to Legion—which is highly unlikely—could have anything at all to do with my pigs!

LEGION: Excuse me! Excuse me! Sorry about the pigs!

BOSS: What do you mean "sorry about the pigs"? (*Turns around and sees Legion*) It's Legion!

TOURIST OFFICIAL: Wait a minute! I thought Legion was a man!

LEGION: This is a new century! Get with it!

SHACKLE MAKER: Hello, Legion. Be good now; and put on these nice, shiny, new shackles.

LEGION: I won't be needing those anymore.

SHACKLE MAKER: What do you mean?

LEGION: I won't be needing the shackles anymore. I'm free. I'm purified. I'm decaffeinated. I've been rezoned—PRIVATE!

TOURIST OFFICIAL: But you're Legion. Surely, you realize that it's your job to be crazy.

LEGION: I'm not crazy—and stop calling me Shirley . . . or Legion, for that matter. My name is Priscilla.

SHACKLE MAKER: So what am I supposed to do with these shackles? I can't put them on some sane person named Priscilla.

LEGION: (*To Boss*) It was a miracle. You see, Jesus cast the demons out of me and into your pigs. That's why I wanted to apologize about the pigs and thank you for your sacrifice.

From WORSHIP FEAST: 15 SKETCHES FOR YOUTH GROUP, WORSHIP, & MORE, by Beth Miller. © 2003 by Abingdon Press.

BOSS: Demons, huh? (*Sarcastically*) Well that makes me feel a whole heck of a lot better!

LEGION: Don't you see—it was a miracle?

BOSS: All I want to know is WHO'S GOING TO PAY FOR MY PIGS?

HERDER: I'm out of a job. Two pigs don't make a herd.

(*The next section should build. Pigs make pig noises during the next few overlapping speeches to add to the confusion. Toward the end, lines overlap as arguments mount to a roar, interrupted by Legion's scream.*)

SHACKLE MAKER: You're out of a job? I'm out of a business!

BOSS: This is a complete financial disaster!

SHACKLE MAKER: Who are we to fear and loathe and run from?

TOURIST OFFICIAL: What about the tourist trade? We had one of the best crazy persons in the region?

HERDER: Who's going to hire me? What "market-able" skills do I have?

BOSS: I wonder whether insurance covers demons and miracles?

TOURIST OFFICIAL: Our village was getting to be almost famous. Not many towns can claim a crazy person running wildly through the tombs.

HERDER: I really miss Muffy and Tiny. . . . poor little piggies. . . .

LEGION: (*Loud scream*)

BOSS: Well, that didn't last long. (*Exits.*)

SHACKLE MAKER: I knew it wouldn't. (*Exits.*)

TOURIST OFFICIAL: He's as crazy as ever. (*Exits with Shackle Maker.*)

LEGION: (*To Herder*) Boo! (*Herder is frightened and runs off.*) Well, pigs, I guess it's just you and me. . . .

SQUEAKERS: The more things change. . . .

JEEPERS: The more they stay the same.

LEGION: Jeepers!

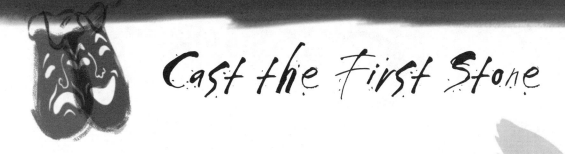

Cast the First Stone

COSTUMES/PROPS REQUIRED: Microphone and envelope for Rachel, videocamera for Daniel. Pharisee and Chief Priest can wear biblical costumes if you desire. You will need several "rocks" of various shapes, colors (one green), and sizes (see the script for details). "Rocks" can be made from Styrofoam, which is easy to cut, shape, and spray paint. The various Emotions will be easier for the audience to identify if each one wears a sign with the name of the emotion on it.

CHARACTERS: Requires a cast of ten: Rachel (a newscaster), Daniel (the cameraman), Chief Priest, Pharisee, Anger, Envy, Resentment, Self-Righteousness, Judgment, Voice of Jesus

SETTING: Scene One takes place at a news studio. Scene Two takes place outside a synagogue near the Mount of Olives, outside of Jerusalem. A local newscaster and cameraman have been sent to get the scoop. A huge crowd, with stones, has gathered.

SCRIPTURE: John 8:1-11

BACKGROUND: This is a retelling of the story of the woman caught in adultery. A crowd gathers to stone her to death. Our contemporary version was written for a youth worship service several years ago. Stonings don't take place today, or do they? This play attempts to examine the stones we carry and how we use them to condemn and wound others. Envy, anger, self-righteousness, judgment, resentment, pride, legalism, and arrogance still kill people's spirits today—if not exactly taking their lives.

DISCUSSION QUESTIONS FOLLOWING THE PERFORMANCE:
- ❏▶ With which character did you identify? Why?
- ❏▶ What surprised you about the portrayal of this story?
- ❏▶ How was the law used to justify what the people were about to do?
- ❏▶ What did the green stone symbolize?
- ❏▶ What stones can you identify in this play that are used to kill another person's spirit, hope, and energy?
- ❏▶ What stones have others used to injure you?
- ❏▶ When have you "thrown stones" and hurt someone?
- ❏▶ What new insight did you gain from this play?

You may want to read the Scripture reference to the audience just before the performance.

DIRECTOR'S NOTES: Entrances need to be on time, with few pauses between lines. Rachel is attempting to "catch" people to interview as they gather outside the Temple. The significant emotional change takes place in Rachel as her awareness of the situation grows. The roles that embody the various "sins" can be overacted to emphasize each character's corruption.

Cast the First Stone

by Beth Miller

SCENE ONE

DANIEL: Rachel, you're late! Here's our assignment.

RACHEL: I can hardly wait. What big news story will we cover today?

DANIEL: You're one of the top "on-the-scene" reporters for *Good Morning, Jerusalem.*

RACHEL: Right! Flattery will get you nowhere. Have you forgotten last week? My assignments included a feature entitled "Unique Booths" designed for the Feast of the Tabernacles. And here's a biggie, the opening of Uncle Bernie's latest lox and bagel shop near the Damascus Gate.

DANIEL: Hey, I love Uncle Bernie's lox and bagels. Where are we headed today?

RACHEL: Nice try, Daniel. (*Opens envelope.*) Great, get the camel. It seems we have to go to the Mount of Olives to interview some itinerant preacher from Nazareth.

DANIEL: It's a great day to get out of town. By the way, who do we interview?

RACHEL: Another unknown, some Galilean named Jesus.

DANIEL: Wow! Rachel, do you realize that this could be your big break! This is no backwoods story.

RACHEL: Explain. . . .

DANIEL: This Jesus guy has caused quite a stir. You didn't hear about his preaching last week during the festival in the Temple? Sure riled the Sanhedrin!

RACHEL: Guess I was so busy with the "Unique Booths" that . . .

From WORSHIP FEAST: 15 SKETCHES FOR YOUTH GROUP, WORSHIP, & MORE, by Beth Miller. © 2003 by Abingdon Press.

DANIEL: (*Cuts Rachel off in excitement*) Yeah. The chief priests and scribes are so agitated, they've got warrants out for his arrest by the Temple police. Rumor has it that they want him dead!

RACHEL: What's the story? Who is he?

DANIEL: The crowds are convinced that he's a prophet. Some say he's Elijah returned. . . .

RACHEL: Another prophet wouldn't have the Sanhedrin sending out death threats?

DANIEL: You are a smart one! Rumor is that Jesus is the Messiah!

RACHEL: Thanks for the tip, Daniel. Mount of Olives, here we come!

SCENE TWO

DANIEL: If you stand here, I can get the synagogue and the crowds in the background.

RACHEL: Good idea! I'll try to catch some of the priests and scribes as they enter.

DANIEL: Interview whomever you want. Maybe we can catch this Jesus fellow when he comes out of the synagogue. Ready to roll whenever you are.

RACHEL: Good morning, Jerusalem. This is Rachel Rosenburg, reporting live from the Mount of Olives. Seems quite a crowd has gathered to hear an itinerant preacher from Nazareth. With me is one of the chief priests. (*To Chief Priest*) Who is this Jesus?

CHIEF PRIEST: He's a nobody, some rag-tag preacher from Galilee.

RACHEL: If he's a nobody, why the crowds?

CHIEF PRIEST: People will go anywhere for a good show. What can I say? He's rather popular with a certain class, if you know what I mean!

RACHEL: I've heard that he's a prophet. Some have suggested that Elijah has returned?

CHIEF PRIEST: People are always looking for heroes, aren't they? Elijah returned? (*Chuckles.*) . . . Next, they'll be looking for the Messiah!

RACHEL: Is it true that there's a warrant out for Jesus' arrest?

CHIEF PRIEST: Now why would we want to do anything like that? Take matters into our own hands? Go against the populace?

RACHEL: What's that you're carrying? It looks like a stone?

CHIEF PRIEST: As a matter of fact, it IS a stone.

RACHEL: Why would you bring a stone today?

CHIEF PRIEST: Never know when you're going to need one. The Law of Moses often refers to stones, so I always keep one handy. Now if you'll excuse me, young lady (*said as a put-down*). I have important official duties to attend to.

RACHEL: But you didn't answer any of my . . .

DANIEL: Rachel, I think you're on to something.

RACHEL: (*Sputters to a woman in the crowd*) Young lady . . . young lady!

DANIEL: I've just overheard a conversation about a possible stoning . . . today . . . here.

RACHEL: You've got to be kidding!

DANIEL: Look around! Doesn't this seem like an unusually large crowd to be gathering. It's not the Sabbath. Why a crowd like this for a "nobody" from Nazareth? Go with your instincts! I'm going to film as much as possible.

RACHEL: Excuse me, I couldn't help noticing that large, ragged rock you are carrying.

ANGER: Someone just cut me off on the road out of Jerusalem. He ran off before I could throw this rock!

RACHEL: If I could just ask a few questions. . . .

ANGER: Out of my way, lady! This is heavy!

RACHEL: What's the rush?

ANGER: People like you really irritate me.

RACHEL: What's the rock for?

From WORSHIP FEAST: 15 SKETCHES FOR YOUTH GROUP, WORSHIP, & MORE, by Beth Miller. © 2003 by Abingdon Press.

ANGER: Take a good look, lady. Wouldn't you agree that I could really do a lot of damage with a rock like this? I should know . . . I gather rocks daily. They come in handy. (*Pushes through the crowd.*) Out of my way!

DANIEL: Hey, I was right! This looks like a set-up to trick Jesus. They've brought a young woman caught in the act. They're quoting from the Law of Moses and asking Jesus whether they should stone her! There's one of the Pharisees. . . . Grab him!

RACHEL: Aren't you one of the Pharisees? May I interview you for *Good Morning, Jerusalem?*

PHARISEE: How flattering! Of course! Let me shake the dust off my robes.

RACHEL: I'll hold your stone for you.

PHARISEE: Please be careful. (*Hands her the stone and starts shaking dust off his robe.*) This is an extremely significant stone—owned by only the most prominent and influential persons.

RACHEL: I don't think I've ever seen a stone like this before!

PHARISEE: No, you probably won't ever see another stone of this caliber. It is very rare—useful for the most subtle attacks. Now, I'm ready.

RACHEL: You are an expert in the Law of Moses?

PHARISEE: What a superfluous question. What law do you question?

RACHEL: The law regarding adultery.

PHARISEE: According to Leviticus 20:10 and Deuteronomy 22:22, both guilty parties are to be put to death.

RACHEL: Is it true that she was caught in the act?

PHARISEE: There's no doubt about that.

RACHEL: Where's the man involved, obviously you knew . . .

PHARISEE: Prominent citizens do not deserve . . . (*Turns to leave.*)

RACHEL: Isn't stoning reserved for special cases? (*He turns back.*)

PHARISEE: According to Deuteronomy 22:23-24, stoning is appointed when the woman is a virgin betrothed to another man.

FROM WORSHIP FEAST: 15 SKETCHES FOR YOUTH GROUP, WORSHIP, & MORE, by Beth Miller. © 2003 by Abingdon Press.

RACHEL: Isn't it true that this practice hasn't taken place in years in Jerusalem?

PHARISEE: I can neither deny nor confirm this.

RACHEL: What if Jesus confirms the Law and lets her die?

PHARISEE: I'm certain that Pilate would be immediately informed that this "new king" is actually adjudicating life and death. He would be immediately arrested by the Romans.

RACHEL: And if he lets her go free?

PHARISEE: Quite simple . . . Jesus would be branded before the people as ignoring the Law of Moses. The Temple police would have a warrant for his arrest. (*He leaves*.)

RACHEL: (*To Daniel*) Did you get that on tape?

DANIEL: Every last scheme, Rachel! This is a trap. We've got what we need. Let's get back to Jerusalem.

RACHEL: You can go if you want. I want to see what happens. I think there's more to this story.

(*Daniel exits*.)

ENVY: What's going on inside?

RESENTMENT: Are they going to bring her outside soon?

RACHEL: (*To Envy*) Your stone is different.

ENVY: You don't have to rub it in.

RACHEL: I meant that it's a rather unusual color.

ENVY: What's wrong with a green stone?

RACHEL: Nothing, nothing at all . . . if that's what you like.

ENVY: It's not what I like! You think I don't wish I had a stone like hers (*Pointing*)? Or his? It's the only stone I have.

RACHEL: Sounds as though you're not very happy with it?

FROM WORSHIP FEAST: 15 SKETCHES FOR YOUTH GROUP, WORSHIP, & MORE, by Beth Miller. © 2003 by Abingdon Press.

ENVY: Are you crazy? Why would I be happy with a stone like this? I'd rather have any other stone here.

RACHEL: Why did you bring it?

ENVY: 'Cause it works. It may not look as impressive, but it works. Besides, I get a lot of sympathy carrying it around.

RESENTMENT: What's Jesus doing? What's his answer?

SELF-RIGHTEOUSNESS: He hasn't said a thing. He's just writing in the dirt.

RESENTMENT: Writing in the dirt? For gosh sakes, can we just get this over with? Carrying this stone around is no small task!

RACHEL: Wow, your stone is huge! It has so many layers. . . .

RESENTMENT: Yep, it has taken me years to accumulate this. Some layers go back to my childhood.

RACHEL: Your childhood? You started carrying this stone as a child?

RESENTMENT: Of course! You think I've forgotten the bully on the playground or the time my mother didn't get me what I wanted for my birthday?

RACHEL: That far back?

RESENTMENT: I could give you details for every layer I've never forgotten any wrong ever done. . . . It has taken years to accumulate a stone like this.

RACHEL: And this stone can be used . . . for hurting others.

RESENTMENT: Mostly its just a pain for me to carry around. But if I throw it. . . .

SELF-RIGHTEOUSNESS: (*Interrupting. Pretending to talk confidentially to Rachel but making sure that Resentment overhears.*) I can't believe people who are so obvious with their stones!

RACHEL: I see that you've brought a marshmallow, instead of a stone.

SELF-RIGHTEOUSNESS: This is a very clever weapon.

RACHEL: Really? It looks so soft, white, fluffy, harmless.

From WORSHIP FEAST: 15 SKETCHES FOR YOUTH GROUP, WORSHIP, & MORE, by Beth Miller. © 2003 by Abingdon Press.

SELF-RIGHTEOUSNESS: On the outside, it looks lovely, innocent enough.

RACHEL: What's on the inside?

SELF-RIGHTEOUSNESS: That's the secret—what's hidden at the center. If aimed at the right spot, (*Demonstrates, aims at Rachel's heart*) it can kill.

RACHEL: (*Nervous*) Thanks. I think something is happening. Got to go. . . .

RACHEL: (*To Judgment*) Whew, at last someone without a stone to throw.

JUDGMENT: It's barbarous!

RACHEL: I agree!

JUDGMENT: Mob mentality! Word spreads throughout the village; and the next thing you know, everyone's gathering stones.

RACHEL: I've seen enough for one day.

JUDGMENT: Did you see that guy with the huge ragged rock? He almost knocked me over, trying to get to the front of the crowd.

RACHEL: How rude?

JUDGMENT: Well, we will have the verdict soon.

RACHEL: I'm not sure I want to stay. It was nice meeting you. (*Goes to shake his hand and is aghast as a stone falls out of his hand. Rachel hurries away. Judgment bends over picks up the stone and puts it back in his pocket.*)

VOICE OF JESUS: Let he who is without sin cast the first stone.

(*Gradually everyone lays down his or her stones on the altar and leaves the stage. For the first time, the audience sees "Jesus," with his back to the audience and a very frightened young woman behind him facing the audience.*)

VOICE OF JESUS: Woman, where are your accusers? Is there no one to condemn you?

WOMAN: No one, Lord.

VOICE OF JESUS: Neither do I condemn you. Go and sin no more.

From Worship Feast: 15 Sketches for Youth Group, Worship, & More, by Beth Miller. © 2003 by Abingdon Press.

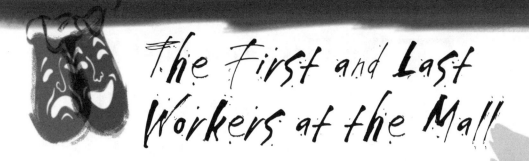

The First and Last Workers at the Mall

COSTUMES/PROPS REQUIRED: Paper shopping bags from various mall stores

CHARACTERS: Requires a cast of eleven: five males and six females—Edward Speilstein (director), Eric (Speilstein's assistant), and nine teenagers who are hanging out at the mall.

SETTING: The play is set at a California mall. The famous movie director Edward Speilstein is hiring extras for his latest movie.

SCRIPTURE: Matthew 22:1-16

BACKGROUND: Whereas the Prodigal Son is often one of the favorite parables, the Workers in the Vineyard is often the least favorite. The moral of the story goes against the American work ethic. The parable says that everyone will receive the same pay, regardless of how long or hard each person works.

Jon wrote this contemporary version of the parable for our annual youth worship service. It was revised over the next year for a drama troupe tour. As new "actors" are recruited for each retake of the scene, the real actors recruited youth from the audience to participate in the play. This interaction with the audience added a new, fun dimension to the performance.

After one performance, a woman introduced herself as a labor union officer. She was very angry with the message of the play. She informed me that this was highly inappropriate for church. She couldn't believe that this play was based on a story told by Jesus.

DISCUSSION QUESTIONS FOLLOWING THE PERFORMANCE:
❏▶ With which character did you identify? Why?
❏▶ What was your reaction to this play?
❏▶ Why did you agree or disagree with Mr. Speilstein's pay scale?
❏▶ What surprised you about the portrayal of this story?
❏▶ What new insight did you gain from this play?

You may want to read the Scripture reference to the audience just before the performance.

DIRECTOR'S NOTES: The acting for the movie needs to be very exaggerated. The first portrayal is with no emotion. The second time, they completely overact being frightened. The third time, they laugh their way through the scene. The final time, they must be realistic. If you are adding people from the audience, the actor (Eric) who brings them onstage needs to tell them how to react. Keep the recruits upstage of the actors.

The First and Last Workers at the Mall

by Jon Stroud and Beth Miller

CAITILIN: Vicki, like, what's the matter?

ANNA: Like, I'm soooo sick of filling in at the Gap.

BRANDEN: No more Ben and Jerry's.

DREW: If I ever see another barrel of Chocolate Fudge Peanut Butter Rain Forest Passion Awareness Delight, I'm gonna hurl!

MEGAN: I'm, like, all scooped out!

ANNA: We, like, have to get other jobs. We're making, like, less than minimum wage.

DREW: Really, I can't like even afford gas for my Pinto-mobile. That's, like, so totally bogus.

MEGAN: How can we get to the beach if you can't drive the Pinto-mobile?

BRANDEN: Really now, Megan. We need to get jobs that pay a little more. I don't have enough cash to buy wax for my surfboard.

MEGAN: Like, how can we surf without wax for your surfboard?

CAITILIN: Did you guys hear that they are closing the mall for like the rest of the day?

DREW: Like, yeah. . . .

CAITILIN: Some, like, movie mogul customers told us, like, they are filming a movie, like, right here at the mall.

ANNA: I wonder if we will see anyone famous!

MEGAN: As if. . . .

(*Speilstein and Eric enter.*)

SPEILSTEIN: This is just perfect! I love the lighting. And oh, these shops. . . . And look at these kids . . . don't they capture perfectly the gritty urban realism of today's youth? This is going to be a great scene.

CAITILIN: Like, oh my gosh! Do you know who that is?

ANNA: It's Edward Speilstein! He is like the most famous director of our generation or something.

MEGAN: As if!

BRANDEN: Whatever.

SPEILSTEIN: Excuse me! Excuse me!

ALL TEENS IN UNISON: Yes?

SPEILSTEIN: I was wondering . . . would you young people like to be extras in my new movie?

MEGAN: As if!

DREW: Like, yeah.

CAITILIN: What is the movie called?

SPEILSTEIN: I call it *Jurassic Park Four: Terror in Suburbia*. This time, the dinosaurs are loose all over the US; and the only way to stop them is for Doctor Rebecca Bennett to tranquilize and tame the mother T-Rex that controls them all.

BRANDEN: Sounds kind of like *Jurassic Park Two* to me. . . .

SPEILSTEIN: Aha! But here's the twist! The dinosaurs are even smarter than they were the last time. Not only can they open doors and escape from cages, they can also drive cars and program computers!
(*To Eric*) Eric, sign these kids up and work out the paperwork.
(*To the teens*) I'm warning you it will be a long shoot, but you will each be paid two hundred dollars. I've got to find an espresso.

CAITILIN: Two hundred dollars! That's like fifty espressos or seventy-five ice cream cones or something.

BRANDEN: I can finally afford some surfboard wax.

MEGAN: Good thing! Like the surf's up, dude!

From WORSHIP FEAST: 15 SKETCHES FOR YOUTH GROUP, WORSHIP, & MORE, by Beth Miller. © 2003 by Abingdon Press.

ERIC: OK, here are some shopping bags. You have to run away from this big blue screen. Pretend it's a huge dinosaur. Crawl through the fountain, just getaway from the dinosaur. Let's get this right the first time. (*Speilstein enters with coffee.*) Mr. Speilstein has returned, so let's get started. Places everyone, five, four, three. . . . Action!

(*The teens pick up their paper bags and half-heartedly scream and walk across the stage—not much emotion.*)

SPEILSTEIN: Cut! Cut!

ERIC: Is there something wrong, Mr. S.?

SPEILSTEIN: Yes, something is wrong! We need energy, fear! This is supposed to be terrifying. Besides, there just aren't enough people, I need more young people. Get me more young people.

ERIC: Right, Mr. S. Whatever you say, Mr. S. OK, kids, you've heard the director . . . terrifying. I'll go find more actors. (*Eric exits.*)

BRANDEN: I think, like, he really likes us.

ANNA: No, he doesn't. He wants us to do it again!

BRANDEN: I thought that all we had to do was run across the screen one time; and we'd, like, get two hundred dollars?

MEGAN: Do you think Mr. Speilstein is dumb?

CAITILIN: Who would pay anyone two hundred dollars just to run across the screen one time?

DREW: Like, yeah!

MEGAN: As if!

CAITILIN: This is all part of being a real actor!

ANNA: Look at those new kids he hired.

DREW: Yeah, like more babes for the Pinto-mobile!

CAITILIN: You wish!

MEGAN: As if!

From WORSHIP FEAST: 15 SKETCHES FOR YOUTH GROUP, WORSHIP, & MORE, by Beth Miller. © 2003 by Abingdon Press.

ERIC: (*Eric enters with Liesl and says to the new actors.*) OK, here are your shopping bags, join those kids over there.

LIESL: Hey guys. What's up? (*The other teens just stare at the new kids, not welcoming.*)

ERIC: Take eighty-two. Remember, gang, terrifying!

(*The teens run across the stage, screaming out of control. Branden jumps into Drew's arms. The scene is fake, overdone.*)

SPEILSTEIN: Cut! Cut! Something is missing. I think we need more actors. Go find me more actors, Eric. I want to make this opening scene memorable. (*Eric exits.*) Now, young people, you're too artificial. I think you need depth. Emotion is never one-sided; that gives a shallow performance. Remember, even in the midst of terror, there is always a lighter side.

DREW: No need to say more. We can do it.

MEGAN: This is harder than I thought!

ANNA: I just keep thinking about the two hundred dollars. Too bad those kids that came later won't make as much as we do.

BRANDEN: Man, he's been hiring new people all day. What's up with that? At least, we're getting paid the full two hundred dollars. Lets' see, two hundred dollars for eight hours, that's twenty-five dollars an hour. Man, and all these other people will only be paid, like, less than that.

DREW: For sure.

CAITILIN: I don't feel sorry for them. We've worked harder and been here longer. None of them deserve two hundred dollars.

ANNA: I'm not sure that we deserve it either, but it sure is more than I make at the Gap. No complaints here.

CAITILIN: How are we supposed to do it this time?

ANNA: What does Mr. S. want?

MEGAN: We've been doing this scene for hours!

DREW: Dang, I think, like, he wants it, like, "humor-some."

BRANDEN: Humor? Like, funny?

FROM WORSHIP FEAST: 15 SKETCHES FOR YOUTH GROUP, WORSHIP, & MORE, by Beth Miller. © 2003 by Abingdon Press.

DREW: Yeah, like, funny, man.

(*Eric enters with Catriona and other youth—from the audience if you'd like.*)

ERIC: Here are more actors. Get your shopping bags and line up with those kids over there.

CATRIONA: Like, this is totally awesome. Like, I'm in a movie. Like, oh my gosh, like, I can hardly believe this. Like, this is top drawer. Like, me, like in a movie. Like. . . .

LIESL: (*Interrupting*) Really, get a life. Just grab your bag and line up!

ERIC: Ready, everyone! Bring some variety to the performance. OK, gang, take one hundred fifty-six. Let's go! And give it some energy!

(*They run across the stage laughing.*)

SPEILSTEIN: No, no, no! That's not what I want! Cut! Cut! Cut! I need a cast worth mentioning. I need more actors! Get on it, Eric!

ERIC: Yes, sir, Mr. S. More actors . . . coming up. (*Eric exits.*)

SPEILSTEIN: Where did THAT come from? This isn't supposed to be funny! This cast is hopeless. Take a break. I need a break.

MEGAN: He's not very happy.

CAITILIN: We can do it. It's just that we're tired.

BRANDEN: Tired? Like, I'm totally wasted. Man, this is rough.

ANNA: I've never, like, heard that making movies was, like, so much work. I had a friend once who was on *Star Search*; but besides that, like, I'm the most famous person I know.

MEGAN: Like, I want to make the two hundred dollars. Lets' just try to get it right this time.

BRANDEN: Why does Mr. Speilstein keep sending his producer out to hire more people?

ANNA: He must have a really big budget. Maybe we should have asked to get paid more?

CAITILIN: Look how excited those kids are to join the cast.

From WORSHIP FEAST: 15 SKETCHES FOR YOUTH GROUP, WORSHIP, & MORE, by Beth Miller. © 2003 by Abingdon Press.

ANNA: Just remember—none of them will make two hundred dollars.

BRANDEN: That's right. At this rate, they'll be lucky to make minimum wage.

(*Laura and Garrison enter.*)

LAURA: Like, hello there! You look horrid! What trauma have they put you through?

CAITILIN: We've been, like, shooting this movie for over eight hours; and my feet are, like, really starting to hurt. And I broke a nail.

MEGAN: These shopping bags are really heavy! (*She tosses a bag, and it is obvious that it is empty.*)

DREW: Whatever. At least, it's almost over.

BRANDEN: I think that he's losing the light. For twenty-five dollars an hour, I'd, like, even mow a lawn or something. Well, no I wouldn't— maybe for fifty.

LAURA: Twenty-five dollars an hour? You've got to be kidding.

GARRISON: It's pretty late in the day. I heard that you are almost done shooting.

CATRIONA: I've been here, like, 3 hours; but, like, I'm in a movie. It's so radical.

GARRISON: How long have you been here?

LIESL: Four hours. It's a drag, but I've heard that we're almost done.

LAURA: Hey, I don't care if it's only for a few minutes. At least, it's experience; and anything I make will be a bonus.

CAITILIN: (*To Anna*) Don't tell her how much we're making.

ANNA: Yeah, she'll be, like, green with envy if she finds out we're getting two hundred dollars.

GARRISON: I can hardly wait! With the money I make, I'm going to start my own Hacky Sack business. My slogan will be "More Hack for your Sack!"

(They all stare at him as if they are thinking, "What a dork!")

LAURA: Garrison, dude, hate to break it to you. But I don't think we're going to make much.

GARRISON: Dang.

SPEILSTEIN: Everybody ready? Let's do it right—energy, focus, stay in character, young people! Give me your best!

ERIC: OK, *Terror in Suburbia,* take two hundred sixty-five.

(Everyone runs across the stage, portraying realistic terror.)

SPEILSTEIN: Cut! Cut! Cut!

BRANDEN: I give up.

MEGAN: As if.

CAITILIN: He's right. We're hopeless.

SPEILSTEIN: Exceptional! Brilliant! That was perfect! Print it, Eric! Put a fork in it, young people, because it's done. That's a rap!

ERIC: Wonderful work.

SPEILSTEIN: You have captured the essence of terror in suburbia. I am indebted to you, the young people of America. Thank you. Eric will pay you.

ERIC: OK, here are your paychecks. The last ones hired will be paid first, and the first ones hired will be paid last.

LAURA: Let's go. Excuse me.

GARRISON: Out of my way. Guess we're first.

CATRIONA: Excuse me! Sorry, we're first in line.

CAITILIN: Why should they get paid first? We've been here longer than anyone.

MEGAN: That's right. We deserve to get paid first.

ANNA: Maybe he doesn't want the others to see how much more we're getting paid.

From WORSHIP FEAST: 15 SKETCHES FOR YOUTH GROUP, WORSHIP, & MORE, by Beth Miller. © 2003 by Abingdon Press.

LAURA: Wow, look! I can't believe what I got . . . two . . . hundred . . . dollars!

GARRISON: More sack for your hack, here I come!

CATRIONA: Like, just walk across the screen a couple times and get two hundred big ones!

LIESL: That's the easiest money I've ever made.

CATRIONA: I'm sure. Like, I'll be famous now, and I even got paid!

CAITILIN: The last two worked about five minutes.

MEGAN: Something must be wrong. They've made a mistake.

ANNA: Does that mean we get paid, like, one thousand dollars an hour?

DREW: Whoa, Vikki! I never knew you were, like, good at math like that. That means we'll get like . . . (*Uses his index finger to pretend to write math in the air*). Let's see, carry the one, times the reciprocal, divided by the matrix . . . like a whole lot of money!

BRANDEN: Dude, it's our turn.

(*All look at checks, stunned.*)

CAITILIN: I got, like, two hundred dollars. But I worked all day.

MEGAN: Me too, I just can't believe this. We should have joined actor's equality or something.

ANNA: Two hundred dollars! Who does he think we are? I mean, we're, like, worth more than two hundred dollars!

BRANDEN AND DREW: Bummer. . . .

SPEILSTEIN: Didn't you young people get your paychecks?

MEGAN: We only got paid two hundred dollars.

SPEILSTEIN: Yes, you received two hundred dollars. Wasn't that the amount established in the contract?

DREW: Like . . . yeah.

CAITILIN: But you paid those losers, like, the same exact amount, almost!

From WORSHIP FEAST: 15 SKETCHES FOR YOUTH GROUP, WORSHIP, & MORE, by Beth Miller. © 2003 by Abingdon Press.

SPEILSTEIN: Don't you concur?

DREW: (*Looks confused because he doesn't understand what "concur" means.*) Like . . . no.

CAITILIN: Mr. Speilstein, we worked, like, so much harder.

ANNA: And so much longer.

MEGAN: I think we're, like, worth more.

SPEILSTEIN: I wasn't taking money away from what I was paying you. I was simply being generous with the others. Is there anything wrong with that?

DREW: Well, like, yeah!

SPEILSTEIN: Why are you complaining? You got your two hundred dollars.

MEGAN: But, like, they got the same as we did.

BRANDEN: Whatever, dude. This is hurting my head just to think about it. You will be hearing from my lawyer.

SPEILSTEIN: You are going to sue ME? Edward Speilstein? For being generous? With my own money? I doubt it!

CAITILIN: What's up with you? I don't get this generosity thing.

SPEILSTEIN: That's obvious. I enjoy being generous. Let's go, Eric.

Chapter 5:
Full-length Play

Chicken Soup at the Bethlehem Inn

COSTUMES/PROPS REQUIRED: Biblical costumes for the entire cast; a scroll for Rahab; diaper bag, casserole dish, and stuffed toy for the Wise Women

CHARACTERS: Can accommodate a cast of thirty-eight. If you have fewer actors, eliminate some scenes or give actors more than one role. See the detailed cast list below.

SETTING: The Bethlehem Inn on the night of Jesus' birth is the setting for the play. After the play, the audience can be led outside, where a live nativity is set up. The cast can gather around the manger scene and lead the singing of several Christmas carols. A soup supper may be served following the performance. During the supper, the cast should stay in character and mingle with the audience.

THEME: Announcing the birth of the Messiah, Jesus.

BACKGROUND: This play is rewritten every October to include every senior high youth who wants a part. The script is written in sections to facilitate rehearsals for a large group in a limited time. Most scenes are self-contained. Only a few characters are in more than one or two scenes. This way, at most rehearsals, three to four scenes can be rehearsed at the same time. Several assistant directors can work offstage, each with one scene, while the director is working with a scene onstage.

The purpose of this play is very different from that of the others in this book. This play is written to include as many youth as want to act. Putting on a fun play to raise money for our summer mission trips has been the main reason for this performance.

CAST LIST

Servants at the Inn
Priscilla
Martha
Lydia
Leah
Miriam
Caleb (bellboy)
James (head bellboy)
Zach (bellboy)
The Cook

The Innkeeper and Family
Samuel (innkeeper)
Esther (innkeeper's wife)
Ruth (daughter)
Rachel (daughter)
Ramona (daughter)
Rahab (daughter)
Rebekah (daughter)

The Jerusalem Players
Joel
Actor 1 (Zillah)
Actor 2 (Delilah)
Actor 3 (Tamar)
Actor 4 (Jezebel)
Actor 5 (Sheba)

Additional Visitors
The Rabbi
Saul Schwartz (young rabbi)

The Roman Family
Octavias Ceaphis
Alexandria (wife)
Julia (daughter)

The Shepherds
Peter (shepherd boy)
John
Nathan

The Relatives
Golda
Sarah
Hannah

The Wise Women
Melchiah
Balthasa
Casparita

The Angels
Hark
Herald

Chicken Soup at the Bethlehem Inn

by Beth Miller

SCENE ONE: PREPARATIONS

(*Martha, Priscilla, and Lydia are on stage when the scene begins.*)

MARTHA: Hurry up! You should be done sweeping by now.

PRISCILLA: Why should we hurry? So she can send us to the dining room to wait on the Romans?

LYDIA: Good point. Let's stay here as long as we can. I swear she will work us to death.

MARTHA: I'm sorry. Did you girls say something?

PRISCILLA AND LYDIA: No, Ma'am.

MARTHA: You know how important it is that the inn be immaculate tonight.

PRISCILLA AND LYDIA: Yes, Ma'am.

MARTHA: And Room 5 needs one more set of linens.

PRISCILLA: I'll go take care of that right away.

MARTHA: Then go help Cook in the kitchen. I don't know what she's going to fix to feed this crowd. It will take a miracle.

PRISCILLA: To Room 5 and then the kitchen.

MARTHA: Lydia, you go to the girls' room and see if the Rosenberg daughters need any assistance.

LYDIA: First, I'll help Priscilla with the linens.

MARTHA: All right, but get to it! And don't loiter! (*Lydia and Priscilla exit as Miriam enters.*) You look bushed.

MIRIAM: I am. If I make one more trip to the market, my feet will fall off.

MARTHA: It certainly is one of the busiest times I ever remember.

MIRIAM: The master keeps admitting more guests and Cook keeps expanding the menu. Then he decides to serve dinner to all those Roman soldiers. You should see the feast Cook prepared for them.

MARTHA: Will she have enough to feed the other guests?

From WORSHIP FEAST: 15 SKETCHES FOR YOUTH GROUP, WORSHIP, & MORE, by Beth Miller. © 2003 by Abingdon Press.

MIRIAM: Depends on how much the Romans eat. It might be a problem. Everything at the market is almost sold out. Just some vegetables and a few chickens left.

MARTHA: These Romans and their censuses!

MIRIAM: Shhhh! The inn is full of Romans. You don't want to cause trouble.

MARTHA: I can't believe they require everyone to travel to their ancestral home.

MIRIAM: I kind of enjoy it. This sleepy town is bustling for a change. And you'll never guess who I just saw at the market.

MARTHA: Who?

MIRIAM: Do you remember Saul?

MARTHA: Rabbi Schwartz's son? The scrawny kid with bad skin?

MIRIAM: The same, well, not exactly the same. You should see him now. Mmmmmmm.

MARTHA: Something worth looking at?

MIRIAM: I'll say! I've heard that he is a rabbi now himself—in Jerusalem, no less.

MARTHA: You don't say. Did he notice you?

MIRIAM: You bet. I made sure of that. (*Leah enters*.)

LEAH: Miriam, Cook's been looking for you.

MIRIAM: How are things in the dining room?

LEAH: The Romans are a rude bunch, and their capacity to devour dinner is unbelievable. You'll probably be making another trip to the market.

MIRIAM: Great! There's not much left at the market—just a few chickens and some vegetables. Well, I'd better get these vegetables to the kitchen. (*Miriam exits*.)

LEAH: Good luck. If you want someone to accompany you to the market, I'll volunteer. I'd rather do that than work with Cook or wait on the Romans.

MARTHA: I've been staying away from Cook. But if you need help, I can send the two new girls.

LEAH: How are they working out for you?

MARTHA: It is so hard to get good work these days. These were the last two servant girls available. They're from Nineveh.

LEAH: Oye-vey. You take what you can get. I'd better get back to the kitchen. Send those two girls as soon as possible. (*Caleb enters*.)

FROM WORSHIP FEAST: 15 SKETCHES FOR YOUTH GROUP, WORSHIP, & MORE, by Beth Miller. © 2003 by Abingdon Press.

CALEB: Have you seen Martha? (*Leah breaks into laughter and points to Martha as she exits*.) I thought we would never be alone.

MARTHA: Well I wouldn't be so sure we are now.

CALEB: Just one little kiss wouldn't hurt.

MARTHA: Caleb, please, not here. You never know when one of those silly young servant girls is hiding around the corner. The guests will be arriving soon, and the master and mistress expect everything in order.

CALEB: Preparations for dinner can wait, but I can't! (*She looks around and gives him a quick peck on the cheek. Then she tries to leave*.) Ah, much better. . . . (*Tries to stop her, grabs her hand*.) Where are you going?

MARTHA: To the kitchen. And you should get back to work. We'll both lose our jobs if you keep this up.

CALEB: We won't lose our jobs. Tonight's the busiest night of the year. The inn is sold out. Good help is hard to find. They're not about to fire us. One more kiss, please? (*James enters*.)

JAMES: What are you two up to? No good, I suppose. (*Martha exits*.)

CALEB: Oh, I've been encouraging the kitchen staff.

JAMES: If the master finds out the kind of encouragement you've been giving, you'll be in the stables cleaning stalls again.

CALEB: I miss working in the stables. It was better than carrying luggage all day. Dealing with horses was better than dealing with fussy guests.

JAMES: I wouldn't let master hear those words, or you won't even be working in the stable. You'll be out on your nose.

CALEB: James, James, you worry too much. You take everything so seriously.

JAMES: Caleb, the only reason you were hired here is that you're my younger brother. So for my sake, just behave yourself.

CALEB: OK, settle down now. I wouldn't do anything to risk your job. What do you need?

JAMES: The guests are arriving. Help the other servants take their bags to their rooms.

CALEB: Got it! Your command will be carried out by the finest of slaves.

JAMES: I would hardly call you a slave—only to your own desires.

CALEB: Ouch, that hurt! (*Caleb exits, while Samuel enters*.)

SAMUEL: James, James, are the guests all properly settled into their rooms?

JAMES: I've already seen to that. Is there anything else?

SAMUEL: Could you please be sure that the CORRECT luggage gets to each room? We wouldn't want an unfortunate situation like the last time. You haven't forgotten?

JAMES: How could I forget, I'm so sorry that my brother delivered the Rabbi's bags to the Romans and a Roman soldier's bag to Mrs. Goldberg's room.

SAMUEL: It was rather funny that it took Mrs. Goldberg two days to discover the error.

JAMES: You had one angry Roman on your hands.

SAMUEL: He accused me of trying to confiscate arms and start a rebellion against the government. No, we wouldn't want another incident.

JAMES: My brother is under strictest orders to be careful about all his duties.

SAMUEL: Thank you. Speaking of Romans . . . how is dinner going?

JAMES: Leah and Martha say Cook is in a twit. Seems like the Romans are eating her out of house and home. She has sent Miriam to the market three times in the past hour. Not much left to buy at the market.

SAMUEL: Why don't we gather all of the guests here in the courtyard. Perhaps we can find some way to entertain them while they wait for their supper.

JAMES: Fine. I'll bring everyone here. One good thing about the Romans— they eat fast.

SAMUEL: Oh, that sounds like Cook. She IS in a tizzy. Where are you going?

JAMES: Off to gather the guests, as you requested.

SAMUEL: James, don't leave me alone with her!

JAMES: (*Hurriedly*) Great idea to bring the guests here. On my way, sir. (*James leaves as Cook enters.*)

COOK: You expect too much!

SAMUEL: Good evening, Cook. How are you?

COOK: What on earth were you thinking? Telling the Romans that you would feed the entire legion dinner.

SAMUEL: It's not a legion—just the local unit.

COOK: You say, "Yes, Your Majesty, we can feed your army." You say this, knowing that the inn is filled to capacity?

SAMUEL: Cook, you are exceptional. I know that you can perform miracles in the kitchen.

From WORSHIP FEAST: 15 SKETCHES FOR YOUTH GROUP, WORSHIP, & MORE, by Beth Miller. © 2003 by Abingdon Press.

COOK: The market is sold out! Miriam comes back with a few vegetables and a scrawny chicken! Vegetables! And the kitchen is impossible to work in.

SAMUEL: I'm sure that you will think of something. You are creative.

COOK: I cannot think. I cannot create. You have stifled all my creativity with such pressure.

SAMUEL: What would I do without you?

COOK: I cannot believe I left Herod's Hotel in Jerusalem to work here! I have half a notion to go back to Jerusalem. (*Leaves in a huff.*)

SAMUEL: (*Follows Cook*) Cook, you can't leave us now! Please!

SCENE TWO: DAUGHTERS, NO SONS

(*The five Rosenberg daughters enter.*)

RUTH: Help me put on my cloak

RACHEL: It's pretty. Did Lydia make it for you?

RUTH: Yes, she's really a good seamstress. She told that me she would help me with my hair. She's from Nineveh; she know all the latest fashions.

RACHEL: I doubt if Mama and Papa would approve of your looking like a heathen from Nineveh.

RUTH: What's wrong with wanting to look fashionable. Besides, the inn is full of Roman soldiers.

RAHAB: You shouldn't even be looking at Roman soldiers.

RACHEL: Rahab is right—good Jewish girls obey their parents. Papa will arrange a match for you.

RAMONA: Rebekah you took my best smock!

REBEKAH: It's too small for you now, anyway. It's time to pass it on to me.

RACHEL: She's right, Ramona. It looks much better on Rebekah.

RAMONA: Rachel, you always take her side.

RUTH: Ramona, calm down. Now you have the perfect excuse to have Mother order you a new one. Look at what Lydia, the new servant girl, just made for me.

RAMONA: Oh, I didn't think of that.

RACHEL: You never think; you just react.

RAMONA: I do not!

REBEKAH: You just did,

RAMONA: Did not!

RUTH: Did too!

RAHAB: Quiet down. I can't concentrate.

RACHEL: What's that you're reading?

REBEKAH: Probably another one of those ancient scrolls.

RAMONA: She gets them from that shepherd boy.

RUTH: That's why they smell so bad!

RAHAB: (*To Rachel*) It's a prediction about a star in the east.

From WORSHIP FEAST: 15 SKETCHES FOR YOUTH GROUP, WORSHIP, & MORE, by Beth Miller. © 2003 by Abingdon Press.

RAMONA: Oh, now she goes beyond fiction—she's reading predictions, fortune telling.

REBEKAH: I think that it's embarrassing to have a sister who reads. Reading is for boys!

RUTH: She gets anything she wants from Papa.

RAMONA: Even Hebrew lessons.

RAMONA: Guess we know who is Papa's favorite.

RACHEL: Yes, but you're Mama's favorite and sure to get that new dress. So just drop it!

(*Samuel enters*)

GIRLS: Papa. (*They gather round him and kiss his cheek.*)

SAMUEL: My you all look lovely tonight! Our inn is most blessed!

GIRLS: Oh, Papa!

RAMONA: Rebekah looks lovely because she took my best smock!

SAMUEL: And you look lovely because you are you, Ramona! Who needs a smock with such a face as yours?

RAMONA: You are the best, Papa! Do you suppose there will be possible suitors at the inn tonight?

SAMUEL: If there are, you will be sure to catch their eye!

REBEKAH: And what about me, Papa?

SAMUEL: Rebecca, you are too young for a suitor.

RUTH: Besides, you'll have to wait your turn. You cannot have a suitor until I am married.

RACHEL: And I will be next.

RAMONA: And then me and Rahab!

REBEKAH: It's hopeless! Why bother with a new smock!

SAMUEL: What are you reading, Rahab?

RAHAB: Peter, the shepherd boy found it in a cave in the nearby desert. He couldn't read it so he gave it to me.

SAMUEL: (*Reads.*) "To us a child is born, to us a son is given." Ohhhhhh.

RACHEL: Papa, what's wrong?

SAMUEL: "A son is given." I doubt I will ever see that prophecy fulfilled!

RAHAB: But, Papa, you have us!

From WORSHIP FEAST: 15 SKETCHES FOR YOUTH GROUP, WORSHIP, & MORE, by Beth Miller. © 2003 by Abingdon Press.

SAMUEL: Yes, my dears, I have you, my beautiful daughters.

RAHAB: Papa, you are such a dear man!

SAMUEL: The regular guests will be here in the courtyard soon. As soon as we can get the Romans out of the dining room, we will serve them supper. So prepare yourselves to greet our guests. I'm sure that there will be some nice young Jewish boys. And who knows? I've been talking with the matchmaker. (*Exits.*)

RACHEL: I have a dress you can borrow, Ramona.

RUTH: (*To Rahab*) I'll fix your hair.

RAHAB: Why? Is there something wrong with it? (*Exits.*)

RUTH: No, I just thought . . . (*Knock at the door*)

RACHEL: Lydia, can you answer the door? Remember, we have no more room at the inn. The inn is full.

(*Lydia enters with Peter, the shepherd boy.*)

LYDIA: This is not a good time. We are quite busy.

PETER: Please, can I see Rahab? It will only be a minute.

LYDIA: The inn is full. The guests will be arriving here in the courtyard any minute. You will have to leave at once.

RUTH: Lydia, you can go back to my room.

LYDIA: But I'm not done with your hair.

RUTH: Wait for me there, Lydia!

LYDIA: Yes, Ma'am. (*Exits.*)

RUTH: (*Flirting*) Peter, what a surprise!

REBEKAH: How are you, Peter?

PETER: I, um, I'm here to see Rahab.

RAMONA: She's busy. What do you need?

PETER: Well, I found this scroll; and I thought that she might like to see it.

RUTH: Here, let me look at it.

REBEKAH: (*Whispers loudly to Ruth*) You can't read.

RUTH: (*Whispers to Rebekah*) He doesn't know that. Keep quiet.

RACHEL: Peter, I think it best if you leave and get back to your sheep.

PETER: All right. Are you sure I can't see Rahab?

RACHEL: You shouldn't be seeing Rahab without Papa's permission.

PETER: I'll leave. But what about my scroll. What did it say?

RUTH: Peter, it was so kind of you to bring this to me.

PETER: Actually, I brought it for Rahab.

RUTH: Never mind about Rahab, Peter.

PETER: Well, what did it say?

RUTH: It's a love story.

RACHEL: Enough, Ruth. Peter, it's time for you to leave.

PETER: OK, but at least tell Rahab I was here and give her the scroll for me? (*Exits.*)

RACHEL: Ruth, you should be ashamed of yourself.

RUTH: Why?

RAMONA: You know why. Flirting with Peter, the shepherd boy.

REBEKAH: As if he even noticed. He only wanted to see Rahab.

RUTH: (*Pouts.*) I just don't understand. Why would he want to see her, instead of me?

RAMONA: Because she is smart and thoughtful and nice and wouldn't try to steal her sister's boyfriend.

RUTH: How dare you accuse me?

REBEKAH: Ruth, you are too much! Pretending to read and telling Peter it was a love story!

RACHEL: Stop. If Papa hears you, you'll never be allowed to have a suitor.

REBEKAH: Please behave, Ruth. There's no hope for me until all of you are married off.

RACHEL: All of you, be on your best behavior. The guests are entering the courtyard.

REBEKAH: This is exciting, I'm sure that there will be some nice Jewish boys!

SCENE THREE: ESTHER

(Samuel and Esther are on stage when the scene begins.)

SAMUEL: And you, my lady, are the loveliest of all.

ESTHER: Samuel, you make me blush! My, the inn looks exquisite.

SAMUEL: Only the best for you, my dear. Martha has done a fine job of putting the servant staff in order.

(Martha and Caleb enter together, holding hands, then quickly dropping them.)

SAMUEL: Martha, Caleb, how are preparations? I must say everything looks cozy?

CALEB: Cozy, yes, indeed, Martha really whipped those servant girls into a cleaning machine. *(Samuel is NOT smiling.)*

ESTHER: Your girls have done an exceptional job with the rooms.

MARTHA: Thank you. I do appreciate your hiring extra help. The two girls from Nineveh are rather slow, but they'll do.

CALEB: We cannot accept any more guests. The rooms are full.

ESTHER: It was quite unexpected when the Roman soldiers showed up tonight for supper.

SAMUEL: Esther, we could hardly turn them away. It would reflect badly.

CALEB: You're right, sir. We don't need any more problems with the Romans.

SAMUEL: Especially after last year. You DO recall the incident with the luggage?

CALEB: *(To Martha)* That was a hoot! Mrs. Goldberg with the Roman's luggage for two days, without even realizing it. And the Rabbi's bag. . . . *(Drifts off, realizing that Samuel is NOT humored.)*

MARTHA: It has put quite a strain on the serving staff. The Romans are being served in the dining hall as we speak. Cook is threatening to leave.

CALEB: The regular guests have all arrived and are waiting to be called for supper, sir. James gathered them all into the courtyard, as you requested.

MARTHA: They are quite a mixed crowd—from Judea, Galilee, and the Jordan River valley. Even some Samaritans!

CALEB: They are all quite well behaved, except for the Samaritans. Now THEY are a rowdy group!

From WORSHIP FEAST: 15 SKETCHES FOR YOUTH GROUP, WORSHIP, & MORE, by Beth Miller. © 2003 by Abingdon Press.

SAMUEL: Martha, could you find Leah to see when the dining hall will be ready for our regular guests? Good luck with Cook.

MARTHA: On my way, sir. (*Exits*.)

ESTHER: What will we do if they aren't done eating yet?

CALEB: I know that Cook sent Miriam back to the market again for more food. The Romans ate more than she ever expected! Boy, is Cook in a tizzy.

SAMUEL: When is Cook ever NOT in a tizzy.

CALEB: When she's asleep.

ESTHER: We were lucky to get Cook from Herod's Hotel. She came here because she thought that it would be more restful, more relaxed.

CALEB: Guess she was in for a big surprise! (*Leah and Martha enter*.)

LEAH: Sir, the Romans have all been served dinner.

SAMUEL: When do you think you can move them out so that we can serve our regular guests?

LEAH: It doesn't look good, sir. They are a boisterous bunch and having a good time.

ESTHER: Have you served dessert yet?

LEAH: They were beginning to do that as I left.

MARTHA: This is taking a lot longer than we had planned. The regular guests are hungry. What should we tell them?

SAMUEL: Perhaps our daughters could entertain them with some song and dance while we wait to clear the dining room.

ESTHER: Great idea. Also, we could introduce the staff to stall for a little time.

SAMUEL: Caleb, Leah, Martha gather the serving staff in the courtyard. (*Caleb, Leah, and Martha exit*.) Esther, see if our daughters are ready to meet the guests.

ESTHER: This is a fine opportunity for the girls to meet some nice Jewish boys from Galilee, Jerusalem, Judea. . . .

SAMUEL: I'd rather you keep the Samaritans away from them. (*Samuel and Esther start to exit*.)

ESTHER: You are so protective.

SAMUEL: I should be. They are lovely girls. I've seen the way the young men look at them.

ESTHER: I do so hope to make a good match for each of them. (*Both exit*.)

From WORSHIP FEAST: 15 SKETCHES FOR YOUTH GROUP, WORSHIP, & MORE, by Beth Miller. © 2003 by Abingdon Press.

SCENE FOUR: GREETING GUESTS

(Music can be playing. All of the Rosenberg family and all servants, except Cook, are onstage. Servants scurry across the stage, carrying luggage, crates, and trays laden with fruit. On the upstage wall, the servants roll down streamers to instantly create a festive atmosphere. The household is practicing to greet the guests who will soon be arriving.)

SAMUEL: Greetings, one and all. Welcome to the Bethlehem Inn. I am Samuel Rosenberg, proprietor of the Bethlehem Inn. This is my wife, Esther.

ESTHER: The Bethlehem Inn has been in Samuel's family for four generations.

SAMUEL: We welcome you to the Bethlehem Inn.

ESTHER: Are you aware that this inn was built on the exact site of the house where the great King David was born? By selecting the Bethlehem Inn, you have expressed your preference for the finer things in life.

SAMUEL: (*As an aside to audience*) Believe me, my wife knows about the finer things in life.

ESTHER: As descendants of the house of David, we welcome you to "royal" accommodations.

SAMUEL: We are all proud to be descendants of the great King David.

ESTHER: We apologize for any inconvenience you might be experiencing due to the capacity crowd lodged in the inn.

CALEB: Those Romans and their censuses really know how to bring a crowd to a backwoods town like Bethlehem.

MARTHA: (*Arguing*) Bethlehem is hardly a backwoods town. We're almost famous—a thriving "suburb" of Jerusalem! We are directly on the route between Jerusalem and Egypt!

PRISCILLA: Ha! (*Mutters.*) A thriving suburb of Jerusalem?

ESTHER: We are here to serve you. We have a staff of capable employees.

SAMUEL: We have a competent staff ready to serve you. James is our concierge. Martha supervises our servant staff. (*Gesturing*) James, Martha.

JAMES: Caleb and Zach are our bellboys.

CALEB: I am proud to report that everyone has been safely checked into their rooms, sir.

ZACH: We possess all the keys.

JAMES: Remember, when checking out, that we do not take Discover, Visa or American Express—only the Master's Card.

From WORSHIP FEAST: 15 SKETCHES FOR YOUTH GROUP, WORSHIP, & MORE, by Beth Miller. © 2003 by Abingdon Press.

CALEB: We only have these five suitcases left. We're not sure whom they belong to?

JAMES: No need to worry, folks. No need to worry about any valuables in these bags.

ZACH: That's right, sir. We went through all the bags and removed anything of value, so they are perfectly safe now.

CALEB: So I'll leave them in the hallway on the third floor, where you can retrieve them.

(*Zach and Caleb exit.*)

MARTHA: Our servants are well trained, polite, and ready to serve you. I am proud to introduce to you the wait staff of the Bethlehem Inn.

LEAH: I must check with Cook and will let you know promptly when dinner will be served.

SAMUEL: Enjoy your meal tonight. We hope to provide some local entertainment for the evening's festivities. Eat, drink, and be merry; for tomorrow you face the only thing as certain as death—TAXES!

ESTHER: We also wish to introduce our daughters. Perhaps they will sing and dance for your entertainment this evening, while we wait for supper.

SAMUEL: We have five lovely daughters—no sons, no sons—but five daughters: Ruth, Rachel, Ramona, Rahab, and Rebekah.

SCENE FIVE: THE JERUSALEM PLAYERS

(All of the Rosenberg family and all servants except Cook and Leah are onstage when the scene begins.)

(Knock at the door)

ESTHER: Miriam, go see who is at the door.

MIRIAM: Yes, Ma'am.

SAMUEL: Remember, we have no more room. Whomever it is, turn him away.

MARTHA: The rest of you, back to work! The food must be ready, and the crowd is hungry.

MIRIAM: Sir, the leader of the group requests that you hear their cause.

JAMES: There's no more room. You heard what our master said. Just turn them away.

SAMUEL: That's right. Tell them to be off at once!

MIRIAM: But sir, it's the famous Jerusalem Players.

SAMUEL: I don't care. Tell them that there is NO ROOM.

ESTHER: Did I hear someone say "the Jerusalem Players"?

JAMES: Yes, Ma'am. Miriam said that they are requesting rooms, but I'll tell them to be off.

ESTHER: Have you no sense boy? This is THE Jerusalem Players, the famous drama troupe. We must find room. Think of what this will mean—people of this caliber, famous actors staying at the Bethlehem Inn!

REBEKAH: Mama, did we hear that the Jerusalem Players are outside?

RAMONA: Imagine—meeting the Jerusalem Players! Joel, the lead actor, is so handsome. I must meet him, Mama.

RUTH: I'm the eldest, Ramona. I deserve to be introduced to him before any of you!

RACHEL: Really, you are always fighting! It's embarrassing!

RAHAB: There's no room, so you might as well just forget it!

RAMONA: We could give them our room, and we could move in with the serving staff.

REBEKAH: Yes! Imagine—the Jerusalem players staying in our room!

RAHAB: I don't like the idea at all.

RUTH: Come on, Rahab. Please? Really, aren't you at all excited about having famous people staying here?

From WORSHIP FEAST: 15 SKETCHES FOR YOUTH GROUP, WORSHIP, & MORE, by Beth Miller. © 2003 by Abingdon Press.

REBEKAH: It is for only one night.

ESTHER: Girls, I don't think that there is any way we could justify keeping an entire drama troupe when the inn is already full.

RAMONA: Mama, maybe they could perform for our guests in exchange for lodging?

ESTHER: Wonderful idea. It's settled. They shall have your room. Lydia and Priscilla, go and prepare the girls' room for our guests.

RACHEL: Where are we going to sleep? You just gave them our room.

RAMONA: We'll sleep with the servant girls.

RAHAB: That sounds like fun!

PRISCILLA: (*Sarcastically*) Fun, right!

LYDIA: (*Sarcastically*) Oh, I can hardly wait.

PRISCILLA: Bet I know who will be sleeping on the floor.

LYDIA: (*To Priscilla*) Certainly none of them. (*Lydia and Priscilla exit.*)

MIRIAM: I will receive them. This is grand. (*Exits.*)

JAMES: I will take care of their luggage. Caleb, Zach, I'll need help. They probably have additional bags with costumes and props.

ESTHER: Bring them to me immediately so that I can give them a proper welcome and introduction. How do I look? This is so unexpected!

MIRIAM: (*Entering with the Jerusalem Players and laughing at some joke Joel has told her.*) These are the Jerusalem Players. This is Esther, the owner of the Inn.

JOEL: Oh my, to find such beauty in a place such as this!

ESTHER: How you flatter me! We are flattered to have you as our guests. Welcome to THE BETHLEHEM INN! (*Joel kisses her hand.*)

ACTOR 1: It is most gracious of you to receive us.

ACTOR 2: This is the ONLY inn in town.

ACTOR 3: I simply must rest and change from these dusty clothes.

ACTOR 4: The road from Jerusalem is appalling. It was a frightful trip.

CALEB: Where should we put their bags? (*Drops one.*)

ESTHER: We are preparing our daughters' rooms for you, our honored guests.

JOEL: Daughters? Are they as lovely as you, Madam?

ACTOR 5: Please be careful with those cases!

ZACH: I AM being careful. (*Drops bags and actors gasp.*) Sorry, sorry, so clumsy.

ACTOR 5: Give me the case. Please just hurry and get me some food.

ACTOR 4: And some wine. I'm told that Bethlehem produces the best wine in all of Palestine.

ACTOR 1: Yes, and some figs and almonds.

ACTOR 3: I need olives and grapes.

ACTOR 2: And pomegranates. I'm told you grow the best.

ESTHER: Indeed, we are known for our exceptional cuisine. Are you also aware that this inn is built on the exact site of the house where the great King David was born?

JOEL: Indeed, indeed, how very impressive. Perhaps in exchange for your unprecedented courtesy, we could grace your remarkable inn with a brief performance?

ESTHER: Oh my, would you really consider performing here?

JOEL: (*Other actors glare at him and shake their heads no.*) But of course, tonight we will perform after dinner!

ACTOR 1: We're not prepared to perform!

ACTOR 5: Now I have to carry my own bags and perform. This is not in my contract!

ACTOR 4: I told you that I didn't want to come to Bethlehem.

ACTOR 2: Remind me again why we've come to this sleepy little market town?

ACTOR 4: The decree went out from Caesar Augustus that "all the world" should be enrolled.

ACTOR 3: "All the world"! It should read "all the Roman world."

ACTOR 2: To Caesar, the Roman world is "all the world."

MARTHA: I'll show you to your rooms. Caleb and Zach, follow me. (*Caleb, Zach, Martha, and the six Jerusalem Players exit. The following three lines are exit lines.*)

ACTOR 5: Please be careful with our bags!

ACTOR 1: Can you believe we have to give a performance?

ACTOR 3: Sing for our supper?

From WORSHIP FEAST: 15 SKETCHES FOR YOUTH GROUP, WORSHIP, & MORE, by Beth Miller. © 2003 by Abingdon Press.

SCENE SIX: THE RABBIS VISIT

(Leah, Esther, Samuel, Miriam, James, and Caleb are on stage.)

LEAH: Ma'am, some bad news—the Romans are still in the dining room.

ESTHER: I thought that you served dessert a half hour ago.

LEAH: We did, but we can't seem to move them out.

SAMUEL: What about our other guests?

ESTHER: They are a patient bunch.

LEAH: We'll need to serve them soon.

SAMUEL: Give them the bill and try to move them out so that we can serve the rest of the guests. *(Another knock at the door)* Miriam, there is a knock at the door. Didn't you put up the no vacancy sign?

MIRIAM: I did!

SAMUEL: Well, see who's disturbing us and promptly turn them away.

MIRIAM: Mr. Rosenberg, allow me to introduce Rabbi Levi, come directly from the Temple in Jerusalem. *(Rabbi bows. Every time he bows, the other characters bow in response.)* And Saul Schwartz, our own Rabbi Schwartz's son.

SAMUEL: Your visit is most unexpected. We are honored. Esther, come quickly. Esther, this is Rabbi Levi, come directly from the Temple in Jerusalem. *(Rabbi bows.)*

ESTHER: Rabbi Levi! How blessed we are to have you dignify our humble inn. *(Rabbi bows.)*

SAMUEL: Esther, you remember little Saul Schwartz?

ESTHER: Rabbi Schwartz' son, scrawny kid with. . . .

SAMUEL: *(Interrupting)* The very same, the young rabbi standing in front of you!

ESTHER: Such a handsome young man, and a rabbi! Are you married?

SAMUEL: Don't embarrass the young man.

ESTHER: You do remember our five daughters? Ruth, Rachel, Ramona, Rahab, and Rebekah? So you and Rabbi Levi will be staying here tonight?

SAUL: We had hoped to, but Miriam tells us that you are full. And we saw the no vacancy sign.

SAMUEL: *(Mutters.)* Esther, we have no room. What are we to do?

ESTHER: Rabbi Saul and Rabbi Levi, we have saved our very own room for you, if that would meet your needs? *(Rabbi bows.)*

SAMUEL: (*Whispers to Esther.*) Our room? Esther, where will we sleep?

ESTHER: (*Whispers.*) With the servants! Samuel, this is a renowned rabbi from the Temple in Jerusalem. And Saul is a possible match for Ruth.

SAMUEL: (*To the Rabbi*) Rabbi Levi, would you honor us with a blessing?

RABBI: The Lord bless you and keep you and give you many sons.

SAMUEL: (*To the audience as he exits*) Oye-vey, if he only knew! How about husbands for my daughters?

JAMES: Caleb, please take the Rabbi's bags to the master's room. You KNOW which room that is? NO MIX-UPS!

CALEB: Yes, sir. Rabbi, I don't suppose you have a blessing for the Romans? (*Rabbi bows.*)

JAMES: This ought to be good—a blessing for the Romans. For their heavy taxes I suppose?

RABBI: God bless the Romans and keep the Romans . . . far away from here. (*Cook enters as Rabbis, Caleb, and James exit.*)

SAMUEL: If he only knew that we have a dining room full of Romans!

COOK: Oye-vey! Do WE have a dining room full of Romans! And they have eaten us out of house and home!

ESTHER: What do you mean, Cook?

COOK: They have eaten everything I have prepared! This is preposterous! I have had enough! I'm going back to Herod's Hotel in Jerusalem.

ESTHER: You can't simply walk out on us now! We still have all of the regular guests to feed!

LEAH: Calm down. I'll take Lydia to the market to get more food.

MIRIAM: Thanks. I don't think I could make another trip!

COOK: And what will you purchase at the market at this late hour?

LEAH: Miriam said that there were a few chickens left and some vegetables.

COOK: And I'm supposed to feed this crowd with a few chickens and whatever vegetables no one else has chosen? I am a world-class chef!

LEAH: Settle down. Why don't you make soup?

MIRIAM: That's a great idea, Cook, you always make such delicious soup!

COOK: (*Flattered*) Really? Well, perhaps. . . . (*Exits.*)

ESTHER: Quick thinking. Thank you!

LEAH: Well, I'm off to the market. (*Exits.*)

From WORSHIP FEAST: 15 SKETCHES FOR YOUTH GROUP, WORSHIP, & MORE, by Beth Miller. © 2003 by Abingdon Press.

SCENE SEVEN: ENTER THE ROMANS; COMPLICATIONS!

(*All the Rosenberg family and all servants, except Cook, Lydia, and Priscilla, are on stage when the scene begins.*)

SAMUEL: Miriam. . . .

MIRIAM: I know sir, I know. Someone is at the door! (*Miriam exits.*)

SAMUEL: Remember, Miriam, there is no room at the inn.

ESTHER: Who could be so rude to come at this late hour?

SAMUEL: Whoever it is, Miriam better turn them away. (*Miriam enters with Octavias and family.*)

MIRIAM: Mr. Rosenberg, allow me to introduce Octavias Ceaphis, come directly from ROME!

SAMUEL: Mr. Octavias Ceaphis, we welcome you to the Bethlehem Inn.

OCTAVIAS: This is my wife, Alexandria, and my daughter, Julia. We are in need of an appropriate room for the night.

SAMUEL: And this is my wife, Esther, and our daughters. Ladies, this is Octavias Ceaphis, come directly from Rome. They are in need of an appropriate room?

ESTHER: Your honor, I assure you, we will find a room for you.

OCTAVIAS: Thank you!

ALEXANDRIA: We appreciate your hospitality.

JULIA: Daddy, what are we to do here?

OCTAVIAS: Julia, please mind your manners. As Roman citizens, we are of a higher status. We must set an example.

JULIA: I don't know why you couldn't have just left me in Rome. The nightlife there is so exciting.

ALEXANDRIA: The night life in Rome is one reason we brought you along!

JULIA: This place is so boring!

REBEKAH: The Jerusalem Players are staying here and have promised to give a performance tonight!

ALEXANDRIA: See, we will find some passing fancy to humor us. (*Whispers to Julia.*) Please be careful what you touch.

JULIA: Why did we have to come here?

ALEXANDRIA: We certainly wouldn't have chosen this town. Your father was SENT here to take the enrollment.

JULIA: What's an *enrollment*?

OCTAVIAS: Caesar Augustus has decreed that every 14 years an estimate be taken of the population and resources of the Roman Empire.

JULIA: Is this part of the Roman Empire?

ALEXANDRIA: Yes, but these people are not Roman citizens.

OCTAVIAS: Rome rules through the kings of the Herod family. Herod is the governor of this region.

ALEXANDRIA: Rome gave Herod the title King of the Jews.

JULIA: Is Herod a Jew?

OCTAVIAS: NO! Enough questions, Julia. (*To Martha*) You do have a suitable room for us?

MARTHA: Yes, sir. Please follow me.

CALEB: I'll come along . . . to help with the bags.

JAMES: That is SO generous of you.

CALEB: Anything to please.

ZACH: Yourself, you mean.

ESTHER: (*Asks audience.*) Would anyone please be so kind as to give up your room for these Romans?

JAMES: Great! Because of this enrollment, the master and his family are sleeping in our quarters. And now they ask someone to move out to make room for them.

ZACH: Guess the Rabbi's blessing on the Romans was short lived. Mrs. Rosenberg, I believe that there is a family over here (*Points to audience.*) who would give up their room.

ESTHER: (*To audience*) Thank you so much. We will prepare beds for you here in the dining room after everyone has left tonight. We certainly don't want to offend the Romans.

SCENE EIGHT: THE PERFORMANCE OF THE JERUSALEM PLAYERS

(*All the Rosenberg family, Miriam, Rabbi, Saul, and all of The Jerusalem Players are onstage when the scene begins.*)

ESTHER: I am so sorry to keep you waiting, but some wonderful news—the Jerusalem Players are staying here tonight and have offered to perform for us! (*Another knock at the door as the play within the play begins*) Miriam, DON'T ANSWER THE DOOR! (*Knocking persists and interrupts the performance.*)

JOEL: I'm extremely sorry, but we cannot perform with that dreadful knocking.

MIRIAM: I'm on my way, and I won't forget that there is . . .

EVERYONE: (*Everyone says together.*) NO ROOM AT THE INN!

ACTOR 2: This is intolerable—constant interruption.

ACTOR 3: An uninformed, illiterate audience.

ACTOR 4: Don't forget—Romans in the audience.

ACTOR 1: We should probably cut all references to Rome. (*Peter and other shepherds enter.*)

ESTHER: Miriam, who are these "fine" gentlemen? (*Holds her nose.*)

PETER: Gosh, golly, Ma'am, we don't need no lodging.

JOHN: No, don't reckon you'd take us in with our sheep and all.

NATHAN: Can't leave the sheep.

PETER: No, Ma'am, we just need directions . . . looking for the newborn king?

ESTHER: And why, pray tell, would you be looking here?

JOHN: Don't rightly know, Ma'am. Just looking.

NATHAN: Can't leave the sheep.

ESTHER: You must leave, with your sheep at once. This is a proper inn, built on the exact site where King David was born.

PETER: Don't think that's the king we're lookin' for? (*Scratches his head.*)

ESTHER: No, that would not be the king. King David is long dead.

RABBI: God bless his soul.

ESTHER: Now be on your way, and good luck finding your king.

PETER: Thank you. Ma'am, for your concern and guidance. Yes, mighty fine lady, real fine, smelled right nice.

FROM WORSHIP FEAST: 15 SKETCHES FOR YOUTH GROUP, WORSHIP, & MORE, by Beth Miller. © 2003 by Abingdon Press.

NATHAN: We can't leave our sheep.

JOHN: She knows that, Nathan.

NATHAN: Do you think that our sheep smell nice?

JOHN: Sheep stink, Nathan.

PETER: We need to leave, boys. We'll just keep searchin', keep searchin'. (*The shepherds exit.*)

(*All the Rosenberg family, Miriam, Rabbi, Saul, and all of The Jerusalem Players are on stage when the scene begins.*)

ESTHER: Oh my, how fortunate that those shepherds were so easily dissuaded.

SAMUEL: I am relieved that they left! Esther, I believe that it's time for the performance.

ESTHER: And now, once again, the prestigious Jerusalem Players' production of the Creation Story.

ACTOR 2: I'm your narrator. It's my task to say just where and how things happen in our play. Set the stage with words, we hope—well heard. No scenery we bring, for the play is the thing.

ACTOR 1: So you shall know, as well as our poor skill can show, whether it is warm or chill.

ACTOR 3: Indoors or out.

ACTOR 4: A battle or a fair.

JOEL: In this, our theatre of the air.

ACTOR 2: To what tonight we represent, a full, attentive ear be leant. . . .

ACTOR 3: A comedy. . . . "The Days of Creation," it is named.

ACTOR 2: Now ye shall gather 'round and hear on this stage, right and clear, how earth began.

ACTOR 3: And then came man.

ACTOR 2: I pray you all give your audience and hear this matter with reverence.

ACTOR 1: Quick, grab the props for the Creation scene.

EVERYONE: In the beginning, in the beginning, there was only God

ACTOR 4: And with God was the Word

ACTOR 1: And the Word was God

EVERYONE: Through him all things were made.

From WORSHIP FEAST: 15 SKETCHES FOR YOUTH GROUP, WORSHIP, & MORE, by Beth Miller. © 2003 by Abingdon Press.

ACTOR 2: In the beginning, God created the heavens and the earth. The earth was a formless void, darkness covered the face of the deep. God said, "Let there be light." God called the light "DAY" (*All capitalized words in quotation marks are to be said by all of the Jerusalem Players.*) God called the darkness "NIGHT"

JOEL: And it was evening, and it was morning the first "DAY."

ACTOR 2: God said, "Let there be a firmament in the midst of the waters to divide the water from the water." God called the firmament "HEAVEN."

JOEL: And it was evening, and it was morning the second "DAY."

ACTOR 2: God said, "Let the waters under the heaven be gathered together." God called the dry land "EARTH." God called the waters "SEAS." God said, "Let the earth bring forth 'VEGETATION.' "

JOEL: And it was evening, and it was morning the third "DAY."

ACTOR 3: This is a bit long. Can we please hurry it along a bit?

ACTOR 2: I'm doing my best.

ACTOR 4: It's been a long day. Cut a few pages of the script.

ACTOR 1: After all, we're not getting paid for this performance.

(*From here on the lines are rushed. The actors are in a hurry to just get through the scene.*)

ACTOR 2: Let there be "LIGHTS," the greater to rule by "DAY" and the lesser by "NIGHT."

JOEL: And it was evening and morning the fourth "DAY."

ACTOR 2: Let the waters bring forth living "CREATURES" and "BIRDS" that fly above.

JOEL: It was evening, morning. . . .

EVERYONE: "FIFTH DAY."

ACTOR 2: Let the earth bring forth living creatures; and then God said, "Let us make . . .

EVERYONE: Man.

ACTOR 2: In our image, after our likeness. So God created man in his own image. The Lord God formed man from the dust of the earth and breathed into his nostrils the breath of life

EVERYONE: And man became a living soul.

ACTOR 2: And God saw everything he had made; and behold, it was very good.

From WORSHIP FEAST: 15 SKETCHES FOR YOUTH GROUP, WORSHIP, & MORE, by Beth Miller. © 2003 by Abingdon Press.

JOEL: Evening, morning, sixth "DAY."

ACTOR 2: And on the seventh "DAY," God rested.

ALL JERUSALEM PLAYERS: The End!

(*The following lines are meant to overlap and be said at almost the same time.*)

ESTHER: Magnificent, magnificent! Wake up, Samuel

SAMUEL: Wonderful!

REBEKAH: Joel, may I have your autograph?

RAMONA: Out of my way, Rebekah. Joel, you were remarkable!

RUTH: It means nothing to be the eldest, anymore. It's simply not fair!

RAHAB: I can't believe this! Our sisters are making fools out of themselves.

RACHEL: I just don't get it!

SCENE NINE: SISTER GOLDA'S ARRIVAL

(*Samuel, Esther, and, Miriam are onstage when the scene begins.*)

(*Knock is heard at the door.*)

SAMUEL: I'm warning you, Miriam. Whoever that is—I don't care if it is Moses or Elijah—tell him there is no room and to be off at once! (*Miriam exits.*)

MIRIAM: (*Heard offstage.*) I'm very sorry. I understand, but I cannot let you in. I risk losing my job. Madam. You really CAN'T come in. Please. . . . (*Golda and family enter, followed by Miriam.*)

GOLDA: I never thought that I'd live to see the day—turned away from my own sister's house. And she, the proud owner of the fancy Bethlehem Inn. No, I never thought that I'd live to see the day!

ESTHER: Golda, how unexpected!

GOLDA: Obviously.

ESTHER: I'm sorry. We really have no room—anywhere. We have even put a young couple from Nazareth in the stable!

SARAH: Is Aunt Esther going to make us sleep with the cows, Mama?

HANNAH: Mama, you promised us we would stay at the Bethlehem Inn.

GOLDA: I'm sorry, my dears. Be good to one another. Remember, sisters should always be loyal to each other. My dear mother, may she rest in peace, tried to teach her own daughters kindness. . . . but it has come to this! Turned out by family, kin, my own sister!

SAMUEL: Esther, seems we have a problem with the Romans in the dining room, I'll be right back . . . (*Under his breath, he says*) . . . *after they leave!*

ESTHER: (*Whispers to Samuel*) Don't leave me, Samuel, you chicken! (*Out loud.*) Golda, I feel terrible!

GOLDA: Imagine—she feels terrible, my own sister turns her back on me in my time of need and SHE feels terrible! I wonder how she thinks I feel? Ecstatic? Overjoyed?

HANNAH: Sarah, do we have to sleep in the stable? Cows are really smelly.

SARAH: Not as bad as sheep. Sheep stink.

HANNAH: (*Crying.*) I wanted to stay at the Inn. I've never stayed at an inn before.

SARAH: Mama, isn't there somewhere else we can go?

GOLDA: I'm afraid not. I'm so glad Mother, may she rest in peace, never lived to see the day her daughter turned her older sister out into the street.

ESTHER: Golda, calm down, I didn't turn you out into the street. I'm just telling the truth—the inn is full. In fact, it is filled beyond capacity. We are all sleeping with the servants. They are sleeping on the floor. We have guests sleeping in the dining room. The only warm, dry place left is the stable.

GOLDA: And we'd have to share it?

ESTHER: With a young couple from Nazareth.

GOLDA: Can anything good come out of Nazareth? All right. Fine. Girls, its looks like we'll spend the night in the stable.

ESTHER: Miriam, will you and Leah make Golda and the girls comfortable in the stables? Take my best quilt for them.

MIRIAM: I'll do my best. (*Golda, the girls, and Miriam exit.*)

ESTHER: Now would be a good time for a miracle. We've waited for years for the Messiah. Why not tonight?

From WORSHIP FEAST: 15 SKETCHES FOR YOUTH GROUP, WORSHIP, & MORE, by Beth Miller. © 2003 by Abingdon Press.

SCENE TEN: IT'S ALL OVER! THE WISE WOMEN AND THE ANGELS

(*Rosenberg family and servants and The Jerusalem Players (22 people) are onstage when the scene begins.*)

(*Loud knocking at the door*)

EVERYONE: There's no room at the inn. (*Enter the three gypsy women, carrying a diaper bag, a casserole dish, and a stuffed toy.*)

MELCHIAH: Where is the newborn King?

CASPARITA: We have seen his star in the East.

BALTHASA: And we have come from a great distance to worship him.

ESTHER: Excuse me. I am Esther Rosenberg, owner of the Bethlehem Inn, and I demand to know who you are and where you have come from?

BALTHASA: I am Balthasa. This is the ravishing Melchiah and the beautiful Casparita—what a face. Lovely Esther lady, owner of the inn, we greet you.

MELCHIAH: We have come from the East, from far, far away.

CASPARITA: We have been traveling for years, following the stars.

ESTHER: There's no room at the inn, especially for gypsies.

BALTHASA: Gypsies? We have been called fortune tellers (that would be true) and Magi (that also would be correct). We have been called wise women—but never GYPSIES!

CASPARITA: Besides, we have no interest in staying at your "inn." We are looking for the newborn child, the King.

ESTHER: We have no King but Herod.

MELCHIAH: But we have seen his star.

BALTHASA: And have gifts to present to the child. (*They hold up their gifts.*)

CASPARITA: We have followed our dreams. We have followed the star. Nothing, not present kings or foolish innkeepers, will keep us from finding the child.

MELCHIAH: Has there been a recent birth?

ESTHER: No.

MARTHA: There was a young couple from Nazareth. She was great with child, and we gave them shelter in the stable.

WISE WOMEN: (*Appalled*) The stables? Tut, tut!

From WORSHIP FEAST: 15 SKETCHES FOR YOUTH GROUP, WORSHIP, & MORE, by Beth Miller. © 2003 by Abingdon Press.

CASPARITA: So you put them in your stable?

LEAH: Yes. We gave them fresh hay and made them as comfortable as possible.

BALTHASA: Thank you. We depart in gratefulness. To the stable! Surely there we will find the King. Thank you. (*The wise women exit.*)

MARTHA: They were very wise women. I'm going to the stable to see. Caleb, are you coming? (*Martha, Caleb, and other servants exit.*)

ESTHER: What if this child is the newborn King? How embarrassing that we did not give them a proper room. I must go investigate what has happened. (*She exits.*)

RUTH: We're coming with you, Mother. (*Daughters exit.*)

JOEL: A King? Royalty? Perhaps we should visit the stable? Players? (*Jerusalem Players exit.*)

SAMUEL: (*To the audience*) If you'll excuse us, we will.... (*Hark and Harold enter.*) Oh my, who is this?

HAROLD AND HARK: Glory to the newborn King!

SAMUEL: Who or what are you?

HARK: I'm Hark.

HAROLD: And I'm Harold.

HARK: Fear not! For behold, I, we, bring you good news. . . .

HAROLD: Of great joy for all people, . . .

HARK: For unto you is born this day . . .

HAROLD: In the city of David . . .

HARK: A Savior, which is Christ the Lord. . . .

HAROLD: This will be a sign unto you: . . .

HARK: You shall find a babe wrapped in swaddling clothes . . .

HAROLD: And lying in a manger. . . .

HARK AND HAROLD: Glory to God in the highest and on earth peace to men—and women—of good will.

SAMUEL: Let us go to the manger. Grab your coats; it's cold out there. Come. Follow me. Afterwards, we can all go to the dining room for supper. I hear that it's Chicken Soup for the Bethlehem Inn! (*All exit.*)

From Worship Feast: 15 Sketches for Youth Group, Worship, & More, by Beth Miller. © 2003 by Abingdon Press.

Drama Covenant

This is my commitment to attend all rehearsals (except in the case of EXTREME emergencies).

I will learn my lines by _____.

In addition, I will work cooperatively with other cast members and the director.

I understand that failure to keep this covenant could result in my losing my part in this play.

I also understand that I must receive permission from the director prior to the rehearsal to be excused from a rehearsal.

_____
(Your Signature)

This is your copy. Sign the copy below, cut or tear on the line, and give it to the director.

- ✂

Drama Covenant

This is my commitment to attend all rehearsals (except in the case of EXTREME emergencies).

I will learn my lines by _____.

In addition, I will work cooperatively with other cast members and the director.

I understand that failure to keep this covenant could result in my losing my part in this play.

I also understand that I must receive permission from the director prior to the rehearsal to be excused from a rehearsal.

_____
(Your Signature)

_____
(Parent's Signature)

Copy for Director

Common Drama Terms

Ad-lib—To utter, perform, or carry out spontaneously

Articulate—To speak clearly and distinctly

Blocking—The process of establishing when each actor enters and exits and where each actor stands at every point in the play; placement and movement of actors onstage

Dialect—A regional or social variety of a language distinguished by pronunciation, grammar, or vocabulary

Diction—Degree of clarity and distinctness of pronunciation; enunciation

Downstage—Toward the front of the stage

Enunciate—To state precisely

Improvise—To perform with little or no preparation; to make do with whatever materials are at hand

Inflection—Alteration in pitch or tone of the voice

Interpretation—A performer's distinctive personal version of a role

Intonation—The use of changing pitch of the voice

Monologue—A long speech made by one person

Off-Book Date—The time when all lines are memorized and scripts are no longer used

Pace—The rate of speed at which lines are delivered and moves are made

Project—To direct one's voice so as to be heard clearly at a distance

Soliloquy—A dramatic form of discourse in which a character talks to himself or herself or reveals his or her thought without addressing a listener

Stage Left—If you are an actor onstage, facing the audience, it's your left. If you are the director, facing the stage, it's your right.

Stage Right—If you are an actor onstage, facing the audience, it's your right. If you are the director, facing the stage, it's your left.

Technical Elements—Lighting, sound, set, design, props, and cost

Upstage—Toward the back of the stage; to draw attention from someone else